A Guide to Usage
for Writers and Students in
the Social Sciences

A Guide to Usage
for Writers and Students
in the Social Sciences

PHILIP and
MARGARET RUNKEL

Rowman & Allanheld
PUBLISHERS

ROWMAN & ALLANHELD

Published in the United States of America in 1984
by Rowman & Allanheld, Publishers
(A division of Littlefield, Adams & Company)
81 Adams Drive, Totowa, New Jersey 07512
and as a Helix book.

Library of Congress Cataloging in Publication Data
Runkel, Philip Julian, 1917—
   A guide to usage for writers and students in the social
sciences.

   Includes bibliographical references.
      1. English language—Rhetoric—Handbooks, manuals, etc.
2. English language—Usage—Handbooks, manuals, etc.
3. Social sciences—Authorship—Handbooks, manuals, etc.
I. Runkel, Margaret, 1906—   II. Title.
PE1479.S62R86   1984   428'.00883   83-19179
ISBN 0-86598-132-9
ISBN 0-8226-0382-9 (A Helix book: pbk.)

85 86 87 / 10 9 8 7 6 5 4 3 2 1
Printed in the United States of America

Contents

Preface

Social science and education seize the interest of many readers. Even the most devoted readers, however, will put aside a book or article when the task of extracting meaning from the printed page becomes too onerous. We hope this book will help writers to avoid some common obstacles to clarity and so enable their readers to go eagerly from one firmly grasped idea to the next.

In reading and editing manuscripts, we come only occasionally upon an article or book whose organization is so faulty that no amount of patching can make it readable. In most cases, clarity is hindered by a few and simple things: strange or vague uses of certain words, a fondness for superfluous phrases, or even the use of unorthodox punctuation.

In our reading and editing, we began keeping notes of things writers repeatedly stumbled over. This book is a compilation of the threats to clarity we found most often. We are happy to report that during our compiling we found several ways to improve our own writing.

We are grateful to Spencer H. Wyant for his critical review of the first version of the manuscript for this book. We are grateful to two anonymous reviewers who scrutinized a later version and made many comments that enabled us to improve it. We are grateful to several scholars and journalists who responded to a request from Spencer Carr, editor at Littlefield, Adams and Company, to tell us what they would like included in such a book as this. We are grateful to those who sent helpful suggestions. Finally, we are grateful for Mr. Carr's own criticisms and for his care in transforming the manuscript into a book.

Philip and Margaret Runkel

Abbreviations

In the text, we refer to the following books by the shorthand at left. At the end of the book is an additional list of the books and articles we mention only once or twice.

AHD

William Morris, ed. *American Heritage Dictionary of the English Language.* New York and Boston: American Heritage Publishing Co. and Houghton Mifflin, 1970.

APA

American Psychological Association. *Publication Manual.* 3rd ed. Washington, D.C.: American Psychological Association, 1983.

Baker

Sheridan Baker. *The Practical Stylist.* New York: Thomas Y. Crowell, 1962.

Barzun   Jacques Barzun. *Simple and Direct: A Rhetoric for Writers.* New York: Harper & Row, 1975.

Bernstein   Theodore M. Bernstein. *The Careful Writer: A Modern Guide to English Usage.* New York: Atheneum, 1966.

Chicago Manual   University of Chicago Press. *The Chicago Manual of Style for Authors, Editors, and Copywriters.* 13th rev. ed. Chicago: University of Chicago Press, 1982.

Copperud   Roy H. Copperud. *American Usage and Style: The Consensus.* New York: Van Nostrand Reinhold, 1980.

Ebbitts   Wilman R. and David R. Ebbitt. *Writer's Guide and Index to English.* 6th ed. Glenview, Ill.: Scott, Foresman, 1978.

Flesch   Rudolf Flesch. *Look It Up: A Deskbook of American Spelling and Style.* New York: Harper & Row, 1977.

Fowler   H. W. Fowler. *A Dictionary of Modern English Usage.* 2nd ed., rev. by Sir Ernest Gowers. New York: Oxford University Press, 1965.

Morrises   William and Mary Morris. *Harper Dictionary of Contemporary Usage.* New York: Harper & Row, 1975.

RHD   Jess Stein and Laurence Urdang, eds. *Random House Dictionary of the English Language.* New York: Random House, 1971.

Strunk and White   William Strunk, Jr. and E. B. White. *The Elements of Style.* New York: Macmillan Co., 1959.

Webster III   Philip Babcock Gove, ed. *Webster's Third*
                       New International Dictionary of the En-
                       glish Language, Unabridged. Springfield,
                       Mass.: G. and C. Merriam, 1976.

Zinsser   William Zinsser. *On Writing Well: An*
                       Informal Guide to Writing Non-fiction. 2nd
                       ed. New York: Harper & Row, 1980.

Special Topics

In addition to entries describing the usages of particular words and punctuation marks, this book contains the following special topics:

Active and passive voice
Audiences
Bring words together
   that act together
Changes in usage
Citing
Connotations
Danglers
Elegant variation
Euphemisms
First person
Infinitive, split
Last name first

Latin
Nouns and verbs
Nouns as adjectives
Overused words
Parallelism
Plurals
Puffery
Sexist language
Usage panels
Varieties of usage
What's that again?
Wordiness

ABOUT has served us long and well. It is as effective as ever. When you find yourself writing *around, as concerns, as regards, as to, as touching, concerning, in connection with, in reference to, in regard to, in relation to, in respect of, re, regarding, relating to, relative to, respecting, vis-à-vis,* or *in terms of,* try *about* instead. It will often be clearer. See also **AROUND, IN TERMS OF,** and **PUFFERY.**

ACTIVE AND PASSIVE VOICE: Not long ago, many scientists—perhaps social scientists, in particular—liked to think that science, at least when properly done, was impersonal. The view seemed to be that the scientific canon encompassed all there was of method—even that one scientist following the canon would discover what any other scientist would discover. The personal attitudes, yearnings, work habits, or other idiosyncracies of the individual scientist were irrelevant. Fitting with that view was the notion that the scientist's writing should give the impression that no human hand had touched the work. The passive voice, of course, does that: "The data were then analyzed."

Many scientists, philosophers of science, and others now take the view that research is an interactive thing. Findings issue from the unique coming together of the investigator and the stuff he or she is studying. What the investigator brings to the interaction—conscious and unconscious assumptions, previous knowledge, subtleties of method, moral attitudes, sensitivity to unexpected facts and phenomena, the culture and historical era, and the like—is part and parcel of the result. When the investigator writes, the same influences are there. If we grant that authors are important parts of the work they are writing about, then it is reasonable for authors and other persons to figure explicitly in the rhetoric. The active voice does that: "Three assistants then analyzed the data independently."

Regardless of where one stands on the objectivity of scientists and other scholars, one cannot deny the rhetorical effect of active and passive voice. The active voice moves with more clarity and vigor than the passive. That can be seen even in short sentences. Compare "Johnson studied burglars" and "Burglars were studied by Johnson."; or "He wrote articles about the neuroses of burglars" and "Articles were written by him about the neuroses of burglars." The active voice avoids ambiguity. When we read "It is believed that a strategy of this sort . . ." we hit a snag. Is it believed by everyone, by some unnamed group, or by the author?

The second edition of the APA *Publication Manual* said:

> Absolute insistence on the third person and the passive voice has been a strong tradition in scientific writing. Authorities on style and readability have clearly shown that this practice results in the deadliness and pomposity they call "scientificese." Some scientists maintain that this style preserves objectivity, but the validity of this assertion is suspect. Now, reputable journals are breaking the tradition with notable success, and writing manuals are recommending a more personal style. . . . An experienced writer can use the first person and the active voice without dominating the communication and without sacrificing the objectivity of the research. If any discipline should appreciate the value of personal communication, it should be psychology. [1974, p. 28]

APA's third edition is more terse: "Verbs are vigorous, direct communicators. Use the active rather than the passive voice." Baker says, "Avoid the passive voice"; Strunk and White, "Use the active voice"; the Ebbitts, "Change the verb or verbs to active voice"; Bernstein, "The passive voice, used without cause, tends to weaken writing"; and the Council of Biology Editors (1978), "Use the active voice except where you have good reason to use the passive."

The passive voice is sometimes handy. But we need not point out the conveniences of the passive voice; scholarly writers already know them too well. See also **FIRST PERSON.**

ADAPT, ADOPT: To *adapt* something is to change it to make it suitable to certain requirements or conditions. To *adopt* it is to take it whole and make it your own.

ADDRESS: The core meanings of *address* are to point yourself or some thing toward someone or something: to address an audience (make a speech), to address a letter to someone, and to use a manner of speaking or a person's title to show that you are directing your remarks to that person, as in "Sir, let me ask you a question." Those meanings get extended to the meaning of directing oneself or one's attention to a task or event. And that sums up the meanings of the verb that dictionaries give.

Recently, many writers have extended the word even further to mean directing anything to anything, or doing something about something, or taking a posture that might lead to doing something about something, or the like. Here is an example:

> Solving problems can be greatly aided by the prior existence of programs, materials, and structures that address some part of local needs.

The doubly extended and vague meaning comes in handy, of course, when writers do not want to take the trouble to hunt for a more precise expression, and the verb has become much overused. Some words and phrases that you may find more precise, depending on the meaning you want, are: *bear in mind, carry out, consider, criticize, deal with, direct or turn one's attention to, do something about, evaluate, go toward, make plans for, orient, think about,* and *work at.* See also **OVERUSED WORDS.**

ADVISER: Both AHD and RHD enter this word with the spelling *adviser* and follow it with the note "Also *advisor.*" Flesch spells it *advisor.* Take your choice.

Intervener also has the alternate spelling *intervenor.* AHD spells it only *intervener,* RHD spells it both ways, and Flesch spells it only *intervenor.*

Convener is spelled by both AHD and RHD with *-er.*

From the frequency with which we see *-or,* we must suppose that some people think it is somehow better to end a word with *-or* than to look up the spelling in a dictionary. We have even seen advertised a cigar named *Relaxor.*

AFFECT, EFFECT: As a verb, to *affect* something is to influence it or effect a change in it. To *effect* something is to bring about, to put it into effect. You can *effect* (bring about) a change in behavior if you can *affect* (cause a change in) motivation.

AID, AIDE: *Aid* is a service. An *aid* is a helpful object. An *aide* is a person who is helpful. When you provide *aid,* you provide assistance. When you provide *aides,* you provide assistants.

ALL: See **EACH, EVERY, ALL.**

AND: If you mean *and,* write *and.* No other word so clearly gives equal weight to the things it connects. Take *along with,* for example: "When she left on the field trip, she took her notebook *along with* her camera." Compare that with "she took her notebook *and* camera." *Along with* implies that the notebook had something to do with the camera. But *and* tells us merely that she took both, requiring neither a connection nor a lack of one. Above all, don't mix connectives in one sentence as if they were all *ands*. Don't write: "She took W *and* X *along with* Y *as well as* Z." See also **AS WELL, AS WELL AS.**

AND/OR: Gracefulness makes writing easy to read; *and/or* is awkward. Strunk and White say it "destroys the flow and goodness of a sentence." Bernstein says it is a "monstrosity."

And/or can almost always be avoided. For "They could have learned about it from the newspapers *and/or* the radio," write "They could have learned about it from the newspapers *or* the radio *or both*." But that sentence also illustrates how *or* can imply *and/or*. Consider: "They could have learned about it from the newspapers or the radio." Wouldn't you naturally suppose "or both?" Indeed, logicians and mathematicians always mean *and/or* when they write *or*, unless they explicitly add *but not both*.

Follett comments:

> The weatherman's "Snow or sleet tomorrow" is no guarantee that we shall have only the one or the other. For generations the chairman has asked, "Are there any corrections or additions to the minutes?" well knowing that there may be both.

See also **VIRGULE.**

ANXIOUS, EAGER: Many people use *anxious* to mean *eager*, but more often in speech than in writing. *Eager* has no taint of distress or worry, but that is indeed the core and most frequent meaning of *anxious*. The usage *anxious to see your* *new car* is unacceptable in writing to 72 percent of AHD's usage panel. See **USAGE PANELS.**

APOSTROPHE: Almost no reader will be discomfited, and almost all readers helped, if you follow the usual rules in using the apostrophe to indicate the possessive: *the experimenter's coat, the audience's reaction, the participants' attendance, James's conclusion.* The possessive pronouns ending in *s* take no apostrophes: *his, hers, its, yours, theirs.*

Actually, no one has yet come up with a rule that decides simply and surely, in every instance, whether to form the possessive by adding only the apostrophe or by adding *'s.* The rule with which Strunk and White and the Chicago Manual begin, however, is to put *'s* onto singular nouns and only the apostrophe onto plural nouns: *the candidate's hat, the voters' choice.* Exceptions are irregular plurals such as in *the children's desks.*

Apply the same rule to proper names. In the singular: *Freud's, Marx's, Jones's, Morris's.* In the plural: *Joneses', Morrises', Schwartzes'.* Some exceptions: *Jesus', Euripedes', Yerkes'.* See Chapter 6 of the Chicago Manual for more detail.

Many sign painters, advertisers, and printers of restaurant menus and letterheads seem to believe the apostrophe has gone out of style: *Kerlingers Steak House, Weight Watchers Special, Julies Beauty Parlor, Composers Recordings, Convention and Visitors Bureau, Misses sizes, Clark Counties only authorized dealer.* Conversely, sign painters often seem to think the apostrophe should be used to denote the plural: *More table's in other room.* Don't use the sign painters and printers as your arbiters. Careful writers still go by the book.

For more on the apostrophe, see **PLURALS** 1. See also **CHANGES IN USAGE** 2.

APPRECIATE: The central meaning of *appreciate*, as given by AHD, is to estimate the quality, value, significance, or magnitude of something, or to be fully aware of or sensitive to something. Possibly the more common use of the word nowadays, however, is to be thankful or show gratitude for something.

It is well to keep the central meaning in mind. To express gratitude for help with a project, for example, you might write, "I appreciate the efforts of John Johnson." To some readers, that will mean that you are grateful to Johnson for his efforts. To others, it will mean that you are fully aware of his efforts, but that you are avoiding saying whether you are grateful for them.

APPROACH: The core meaning of the noun *approach* is an access, a way of reaching a person or a destination—a road or walkway. That meaning has been extended to the use of *approach* to mean the *method* of doing almost anything. RHD's illustration is "His approach to all problems was to prepare an outline." A still further extension takes us to a meaning now seen fairly often: a viewpoint from which something is to be studied or discussed, as in this excerpt from an article about philanthropic foundations:

> Each foundation has its own program interests. Proposals submitted to a foundation are reviewed against these program interests by program officers. You will find differences of approach among program officers in the same foundation; in the larger ones, these can be important differences.

Since *approach* has been extended to so many meanings, it becomes too handy a word and gets overused. The more it is overused, the more vague it becomes and the less necessary it is. Several words, including *approach*, can be omitted from the excerpt about foundations without changing the meaning:

> Each foundation has its own program interests, and program officers review proposals against them. You will find differences,

however, among program officers in the same foundation; in the larger ones, the differences can be important.

Here is another example: "anyone interested in the internal change team approach to organizational change" can be conveyed more briefly: "anyone interested in using internal change teams in organizations."

In the sense of method, you might find one of these words to be closer to the meaning you want: *means, method, procedure, strategy, tack, tactic, technique, way.*

In the sense of viewpoint, try one of these: *assumption, conception, consideration, idea, image, impression, notion, opinion, outlook, perspective, persuasion, point of departure, sense, slant, standpoint, surmise, theory, thesis, values, viewpoint.*

See also **OVERUSED WORDS** and **WORDINESS.**

AREA: See **OVERUSED WORDS.**

AROUND: Prepositions are wonderfully useful words; they distinguish many kinds of connections between other words. But they can do that only if they are used with discrimination. Recently, *around* has been appearing where other prepositions are customary. Here are some examples:

> The plan was based *around* an issue [Make it instead "*on* an issue."]
>
> . . . efforts to connect the groups *around* common concerns. [Make it "*through* their common concerns" or "*on the basis of* their common concerns."]
>
> We should encourage research *around* the variables mentioned earlier. [Make it "*on* the variables."]
>
> The measurement of student achievement *around* standardized achievement tests is ill advised for another reason. [Make it "*with*" or "*by* standardized achievement tests."]

And to speak of things *centering around* something else, Follett says, is to try to put the core around the apple. Let things center *on, upon, in,* or *at.* See also **ABOUT, ONE ON ONE,** and **SPEAK TO.**

AS, LIKE: See **LIKE, AS.**

AS SUCH: Sometimes *as such* is used to mean "in itself," as in "The position, as such, did not give him much authority." That usage is almost always clear. *As such* is also used to mean, as AHD puts it, "as being the person or thing implied or previously mentioned." That use of the phrase is trickier; your context must point clearly to the thing previously mentioned. Here is a clear example:

> Alfred was acclaimed the leader. As such, he was immediately part of a new communication network.

Here is an unclear example:

> Recently elaborated models offer a partial answer to this question; they seek to provide a more realistic description of the process by which social research is *actually* conducted than that implied by the conventional "rational" model of the research process. As such, these models establish . . .

To what does *as such* refer? After some puzzling, we concluded that the author was referring to "Recently elaborated models" at the beginning of the previous sentence. That is too far back for easy reference. In addition, the sentence does not prepare us for a reference about *being.* In the first example, *as such* refers to the state of *being* the leader. In the second example, however, the first sentence does not tell us about models *being* something; instead, it tells us about models *doing* something: offering and seeking. With those verbs in mind, we are ill prepared for *as such.* Without any alteration of the first sentence, the author could have written clearly by foregoing *as such* altogether and using a repetition of words to show the reference: "These more realistic models establish . . ." See also **SUCH.**

ASTERISKS: Put the sending asterisk right *after* the word, phrase, or sentence on which you want to comment. Put the receiving asterisk right *before* the comment at the bottom of the page.* Use asterisks *only* to send the reader to footnotes, and for no other purpose.

AS WELL, AS WELL AS: In some sentences, *as well* and *as well as* seem to say little more than *and.* For example: "The beans were good and the potatoes as well." That says little more than that both the beans and the potatoes were good. Perhaps the diner was served the beans before the potatoes, perhaps not. *As well* doesn't suggest any distinction between the beans and the potatoes.

Now consider "He gave her the beans, and the potatoes as well." there the beans seem to have been given under a different understanding from the potatoes. The sentence says that he gave her *not only* the beans, *but also* the potatoes. That is, the potatoes were not part of the ordinary expectations that brought her the beans.

If you want to mean more than *and,* use *A, and B as well* to mean *not only A, but also B.* Use *A as well as B* to mean *A and not only B*; that is, *not only B, but also A.* The two phrases point in opposite directions.

Since you cannot always depend on the directional meaning of *as well* or *as well as* to stand out strongly, you can only reread with extra care any sentence in which you have used one of those phrases. Pretend you have never seen the sentence before, and listen carefully for its meaning. See also **AND.**

------

*Like this.

AT LEAST: See **MAXIMUM, MINIMUM.**

ATTEMPT

1. Most scholarly writers try to write with some modesty. But the yin and yang are with us in every human endeavor, including writing. The wish to be modest is matched by the wish to be immodest. Following suit, we urge writers to be more modest under **PUFFERY,** but in several other places we urge them to be less modest—see **AUDIENCES, FIRST PERSON,** and **THEORY.**

Scholarly writers sometimes put on the garments of modesty by refraining from claiming success in their endeavors, leaving that judgment to their peers. Their modesty can go as far as not even claiming to explain, outline, display data, test a relation, or reach a conclusion, but only to *attempt, try, endeavor,* or *seek* to do so. That seems to us overmodest.

Furthermore, when authors tell us they *attempted* to study something, we can only suppose they will tell us later how they failed, since the word *attempt* implies something less than success, or at least leaves the matter chancy. That kind of introduction makes us reluctant to read further. Grumbling, however, we usually do read on, because we have learned that authors who start out that way usually don't mean what they say; their modesty is sham. We prefer authors to tell us straightforwardly that they will explain, compare, test, or whatever—not that they will merely try to do so—and let us judge their results for ourselves. That seems to us the more honest modesty.

2. Regardless of questions of modesty, the word *attempt* seems to us overused. See **OVERUSED WORDS** for synonyms.

AUDIENCES: Whoever the audience, your first task is to capture their interest. Readers want to know first: What is this article or book about? Should I go on reading it? Your task is not to convince uninterested readers that they ought to have an interest in your subject, but to tell readers who have an interest, or a beginning of one, how your article or book will communicate with their interest.

Readers want to know next: In what style is the author going to deal with this subject? Is the author writing as authority, empirical researcher, onlooker, synthesist, theorist? Descriptively, exhortingly, factually, frivolously, humorously, in depth, judgmentally, moralistically, playfully, soberly, solemnly, superficially, tongue-in-cheek? From the words you use in your first page or two, the way you order the words in syntax, the length of your sentences, and all the other features of your writing, readers judge whether your style of dealing with your subject matches their own sense of appropriateness. Their reaction to your style determines whether they will go on reading.

Clarity comes first. Regardless of other features of style— sobriety, humor, abstractness, concreteness, or whatever— readers will stop reading what they cannot track. Beyond clarity, however, different audiences have different expectations about style. Most newspaper readers probably would become impatient with an article that read like the *Scientific American,* and just as probably most readers of the *Scientific American* would become impatient with an article there that read like a newspaper. One style is not "better" than another in any absolute way. Different styles of writing match the different purposes of the different publications.

You will, of course, bend your style more or less toward the kind of writing you have seen published for the kind of audience you want to reach. If you are writing for the *Psychological Review,* you will be unlikely to choose a breezy style, regardless of whether you think that journal would benefit from some fresh air. For one thing, editors will reject a paper whose style is too far from their custom. For another thing, even if the paper were printed, the readers' attention would be distracted from what you wrote to how you wrote it. You will not be listened to very seriously if you go to cocktails at the embassy in a bathing suit, nor if you go to a beach party in a tuxedo.

The converse is also true. You can be so much like everyone else that you become a dull repetition. That fate falls upon too many graduate students. Some try so hard to write like members of their dissertation committee that they lose their own identity, and it sometimes takes them years to recover it. Writing is a personal and inner thing. If you try to write with someone else's pen, you will often scritch when you ought to scratch.

There is no best way to write, no universally appealing style. No matter how you write, you will neither please everyone nor displease everyone. Writers to whom readers want to return write with some boldness. But if you write with any distinction at all, some readers will be delighted and others repelled. If you change, others will be delighted and still others repelled. Whether you will turn away some readers is not a choice you have. The *kind* of reader you turn away, however, is to some degree within your power. Some academic readers are annoyed by the use of "I," some by the passive voice, some by informal sentences like "Get as much clarity as you can," and others by formal sentences like "The acquisition of lucidity should be maximized." Whom would you rather annoy? The choice is yours.

See also **ACTIVE AND PASSIVE VOICE; ATTEMPT; CHANGES IN USAGE; FIRST PERSON; THEORY; THIS, THAT;** and **VARIETIES OF USAGE.**

BAD: see **GOOD.**

BADLY: When you come in out of the rain, do you say you *feel wetly?* When you come in out of the cold, do you *feel* *coldly?* When you are happy, do you *feel goodly?* Does he *appear healthily?* Do fir trees *grow highly?* Does the butter *taste rancidly?* Does he *look handsomely?* In sum, don't write that you *feel badly* unless your sense of touch is defective.

The verbs in italics in the previous paragraph are all acting as "linking verbs." They function in the same way as *is:* "She is wet. She feels wet." They connect the subject of a sentence with a word or phrase telling the condition or state of the subject. An adjectival form, therefore, not an adverbial form, should follow the verb.

If you taste badly, you are less likely to notice when things taste bad. Everyone sees badly in a snowstorm, but farmers and skiers can see good in a snowfall when motorists see only bad. If lovers or safecrackers feel badly, they have reason to feel bad about it.

Follett suggests some ways of avoiding the choice between *bad* and *badly: feel sorry, feel regret, have qualms, be uneasy.*

RHD says that both *feel bad* and *feel badly* occur in standard English, but that *feel bad* is usually preferred in formal writing. The usage note in AHD says that "*bad,* not *badly* is the proper form following linking verbs such as *feel* and *look.*" Seventy-five percent of AHD's usage panel say to use *bad* in writing (see **USAGE PANELS**). AHD says that "*feel badly*" is "informal." Our own strong impression, however, is that far from allowing themselves to be informal, the people we know who use *feel badly* are trying all too hard to be formal.

BASED ON: See **DANGLERS** 2.

BASIS, BASIC, BASICALLY: A *basis* is the bottom or base of something. Other things are erected on it. What is *basic* lies at the bottom, physically, in logic, or figuratively.

If someone writes "Basically, the problem was to get the work done quickly" and means that speed was the most urgent thing at the moment, then the writer is stretching *basically* too far. What is basic is not merely urgent or important; it is what all else depends on or builds on.

Another example: "Basically, the group did not have the skill to make a a clear decision." Some writers would mean by such a sentence merely that *the truth was* or *the plain fact was* or *the main thing was* or *the point I want to emphasize is* that the group did not have the skill to make clear decision. Those meanings are not best conveyed by *basically*. Other writers might mean that the group could not make a clear decision without the necessary skill, and the group did not have it. But what is necessary is not always basic. The third floor is necessary to the fourth floor, but it isn't the foundation. If the idea of a basis is wanted, the sentence might be rewritten: "A clear decision is built on a base of adequate skills, and the group did not have it." or "The group lacked the basis of a clear decision: adequate skill." Or "The group's decisions were unclear because of a basic lack: it did not have the skill."

The nearest synonyms to *basis* are *base, bottom, footing, foundation*. In conceptual matters, some synonyms are *ground, origin, root, spring*. Two adjectives are *fundamental, radical*.

When you mean *chiefly, predominantly, most of the time, generally*, or *usually*, use those words instead of *basically*.

Orally, *basically* has become almost as meaningless as the *you know* with which many people sprinkle their speech. We heard an interviewee on the television say, "Basically, dyslexia was discovered in 1898."

See also **DANGLERS** 2 and **WORDINESS** 4.

BECAUSE: See **REASON IS BECAUSE** and **THIS IS BE- CAUSE.**

BELIEVE, FEEL, THINK: These three words go more or less like this:

> Though we *believed* our moral stance to be the right one, and though we had *thought* through in detail the steps we would take, nevertheless we *felt* some anxiety as we went into the first meeting.

The dictionaries agree on the core meanings. *Believe:* to accept as true, real, or honestly offered; to have faith. *Feel:* to perceive through touch or another sense; to be aware of an emotion; to have one's sensibilities affected; to have a vague overall impression. *Think:* to have as a thought; to reason about or ponder; to judge; to visualize. These sentences may help:

> I believe I have eaten something poisonous.
> I feel as if I have eaten something poisonous.
> I think I have eaten something poisonous.

The first conveys a conviction, the second a sensation in the stomach, and the third a coolly considered hypothesis.

The dictionaries also agree that people sometimes use one word in the core sense of another. Careful writers, however, can help their readers to catch their meaning by distinguishing among the three words.

BOSS: Some people think *boss* is nonstandard or slang. It is, in fact, part of standard usage and has been for a long time. Use it when it fits.

BOTH

> This paper develops and duplicates some work in Glanville (1979). However, the intentions in both papers are quite different.

The author did not actually mean that the intentions in his paper were different and so were those in Glanville's. He meant that the intentions in *the two* papers were different, or that the intentions differed *between* the papers.

BRING, TAKE: In general, things are *brought to* you and *taken from* you. *Bring* and *take* match *come* and *go*. *Bring* tells the reader that things move toward you:

> He *brought* the report with him when he *came* to the meeting. (I was waiting there.)
>
> She *brought* it with her as she crossed the room. (She was walking toward me.)

Or that they arrive with you:

> I had *brought* the report with me to the meeting. (I had it when I arrived).

> *Take* tells the reader that things move away from you:

> She *took* the report with her when she *went* to the meeting. (I wasn't there.)
>
> He *took* it with him as he crossed the room. (He was walking away from me.)

Or that they depart with you:

> I *took* the report with me to the meeting. (I had it with me when I departed to go to the meeting.)

BRING WORDS TOGETHER THAT ACT TOGETHER: In his article on "ambiguity," Fowler quotes from an "old grammarian" the golden rule of writing: "that the words of members most nearly related should be placed in the sentence as near to one another as possible, so as to make their mutual relation clearly appear." That was written a long time ago, but the rule still holds.

1. Some disjunction of phrases that ought to work together results from sheer carelessness. Authors of books on English composition like to quote the advertisement of a "piano for sale by man leaving city in rosewood case with carved legs." Fowler (under "ambiguity") gives these gems: "Please state from what date the patient was sent to bed and totally incapacitated by your instructions." "I can recommend this

candidate for the post for which he applies with complete confidence." And this, apparently the title of a memorandum: "To ask the Minister of Agriculture if he will require eggs to be stamped with the date when they are laid by the farmer."

2. In a sentence of any length, it is often impossible to put every word close to every other it works with. When that is the case, it is usually helpful to inspect the main structure of the sentence. Consider this sentence from a newspaper: "Logs must be stored properly—split into small pieces, stacked off the ground, and covered—to dry." Upon reaching the word *properly*, the writer apparently felt an urge to explain what he or she meant by it. That left *to dry* hanging awkwardly at the end. Since the main idea in the sentence was to explain something about drying the logs, the sentence would have read more easily if *to dry* had been closer to the main subject and verb: "Logs must be stored properly to dry; they should be split into small pieces, stacked off the ground, and covered."

Sometimes writers feel an urge to get all their qualifications into the sentence before the word to be qualified. One way writers do that is to put a string of adjectives before a noun. Suppose you read this much of a sentence: *There would be more emphasis on* . . . You expect the next word to tell you what there would be more emphasis on. But that is not what readers encountered in this sentence from an educational journal: "There would be more emphasis on large group question and answer recitation."

If hyphens are used to make one adjective from three words and to pull the eye along, *recitation* can be put closer to its preposition: "There would be more emphasis on question-and-answer recitation in large groups." Or even: "There would be more emphasis on recitation by question and answer in large groups."

See also **HYPHENS** and **NOUNS AS ADJECTIVES.**

3. Breaking up prepositional phrases seems to have become almost a fad. Whatever may be driving writers to do it, it makes for awkward reading: "We engaged in careful planning of, and resource allocation to, our activities." Make it instead: "We planned our activities and allocated resources to them carefully." Or, if strong emphasis on care is wanted; "We planned our activities carefully and allocated resources to them carefully."

Another example: "This posture contributes to, and is in part a product of, the dissolution of the conventional belief system." Since the author used the conjunction *and*, he or she presumably wanted the posture's contribution to the dissolution to have equal emphasis with the dissolution's production of the posture. So a direct rearrangement of the sentence goes like this: "This posture contributes to the dissolution of the conventional beliefs and is in part of product of it." But the first part of the sentence is long enough so that the subject of *is* and the referent of *it* are not immediately obvious. Furthermore, the two parts of the sentence move in opposite directions, and that makes parallelism difficult. It seems better to use two sentences or a compound sentence like this one: "This posture contributes to the dissolution of the conventional beliefs and, at the same time, that very dissolution contributes to the posture." See **PARALLEL CONSTRUCTION.**

The author of this sentence got lost in the middle: "Unobtrusive measures seem to be associated with and induce a different set toward data collection than is true for self-report measures." Associated with what?

Some authors have a penchant for separating not only words that belong together, but even syllables that belong together. Instead of *pretest and posttest*, for example, they write *pre- and posttest*. That strikes us as deep-dyed pedantry.

4. Discard the rule to bring words together that act together when you want dramatic emphasis: "But, in a larger sense,

we cannot dedicate—we cannot consecrate—we cannot hallow—this ground."

BURGEON: The core meaning of *burgeon* is to sprout, to begin to grow, to put forth new buds or greenery. It has been extended to mean to grow or increase suddenly or very rapidly. But no dictionary includes simply *increasing* or *spreading* as one of its meanings.

CAN, MAY: The core meaning of *can* is to have the ability or capability. Persons *can* do something when they are able to do it: "Can he lift that heavy box?" A thing can be done, too, if it is in the nature of things for it to be *possible*—if nature has the capability, so to speak: "Three trials can be run in an afternoon. The actual scores can range from zero to 100."

May has two core meanings: (a) Persons *may* do something when they are given permission: "We may travel within our country without passports." That is, we are permitted to do so. (b) A thing *may* happen when we are uncertain whether it will happen: "She may or may not decide to go."

Informal or colloquial usage sometimes puts *can* in place of *may* in a question such as "Can I have a piece of candy?" But neither informal nor colloquial usage puts *may* in place of *can*. If we hear "May he lift that heavy weight?" We interpret it as a request for permission for him to try, not as a request for information about his ability.

Only Webster III mentions the possibility of putting *may* in place of *can*, but marks it "archaic." Oddly enough, this archaic usage does appear nowadays in some scholarly writing, perhaps especially in that of social scientists. Here are some examples:

> Although many researchers use the two-dimensional typology, it is clear that the three-dimensional typology may be logically derived from it.

That author clearly means that it is logically *possible* to derive the three-dimensional typology. He clearly does not mean that someone is permitting him to make the derivation, and he clearly is in no doubt whether he can carry through the derivation. He should have written *can be logically derived*, not *may be*.

> References to those resources may be found in the technical paper . . .

Does that author write *may* because he is unsure whether the references actually appear in the technical paper? Such carelessness seems unlikely. Is he giving the reader permission to look there? Such impertinence seems unlikely. He should have written *can be found*.

> As a consequence of Equation 4, the difference D_1 may be expressed as . . .

Does that writer mean that he is permitting us to express the difference in the way he proposes? Hardly. Does he mean that he is uncertain whether the difference is expressible in that matter? Hardly. He means *can*.

Even writers of dictionaries fall into this strange usage. AHD distinguishes clearly the core meanings of *can* and *may*; yet the writer of the entry in AHD for *rhetorical question* defines it as "a question . . . to which only one answer *may* be made" (italics ours).

CAUCASIAN: In 1975, Blumenbach proposed his classification of humankind into five races, one of which he named *Caucasian*. Anthropologists and geneticists long ago found Blumenbach's scheme inadequate and dropped his five labels, including *Caucasian*, from their technical vocabulary. In 1962, Dobzhansky (pp. 263—65) offered a list of 34 races; *Caucasian* was not among them. As a scientific term, *Caucasian* is as out of date as *bilious*. But Dobzhansky's terms are too precise and too unfamiliar to be used without explanation to readers outside anthropology. For general use, *white* is good enough.

The population geneticist Richard Lewontin writes:

> The problem with these categories is that there are too many contradictions between the different ways of dividing human races. . . . The effort to build a more and more complex set of categories of human types that would correspond to the incredible variety of human beings finally fell under its own weight. . . . Anthropologists no longer try to name and define races and subraces. . . . The notion that there are stable, pure races that only now are in danger of mixing under the influence of modern industrial culture is nonsense [1982, pp. 111—12].

CHANGES IN USAGE: Language changes; we won't argue about that. But a couple of over-simple notions need to be got out of the way. The first is that "the language" changes as if it has a will of its own, and individuals can only submit. The second is that "the language" is a monolithic thing—that if you hear or read a new usage, it must be that "everybody" is using it.

1. The language changes because individual speakers and writers use new words, or old words in new ways, or new idioms, or new syntax. Sometimes, one or a few persons introduce a new word or a new usage that gains wide acceptance. For example, a few manufacturers and advertisers have put words into the language. For a long time, an automobile built to seat two people comfortably was a *coupe;* now it is a *sports car.* A *talking machine* became a *victrola* (originally a trade name) and later a *hi-fi.*

A few psychologists have given several words to general usage, though their original technical meanings have gotten lost. For some people, *identify with* means about the same as like, admire, or sympathize; to have a *complex* is to be sensitive to something; *intelligence* means what your parents hope you gain from school. A few computer experts have given us *input, output,* and *interface.*

Airlines have done their part. Once we departed *from* Chicago, flying *on* one of United's airplanes. Now we depart Chicago, flying United. (Are prepositions disappearing? Perhaps someday we will sit table, go town, and fall love.)

Gelett Burgess single-handedly gave us *blurb*. Lewis Carroll single-handedly gave us *chortle*.

People also resist using new words. Edison called his new incandescent device an electric *lamp*, and one brand was advertised for years as *Mazda Lamps*. Yet individuals by the thousands and then millions chose to call those devices *bulbs*. They didn't hold a convention or exchange scholarly papers; they simply neglected to say *lamp*. Early automobile manufacturers offered us the term *horseless carriage*. People might have accepted that, perhaps shortening it to *horseless*, as the British shortened *wireless telegraphy* to *wireless* and the Americans shortened *radiotelegraphy* to *radio*. But individuals by the thousands and millions declined to use *horseless carriage* and instead adopted *automobile* (a more scholarly word) and *car*.

You are free to accept or reject a new usage as you see fit. When you encounter a new word or usage several times in conversation or in print, you cannot know whether you are witnessing a fad or a change that will become standard and remain so for the rest of your life. If you like the new term, you can pick it up for your own use, or you can decline it. Often it comes down to whether you want to be up to the minute or whether you want to maintain your old habits. Each choice has its advantages and disadvantages. For some of Zinsser's choices, see **USAGE PANELS.**

What seems to be a new word or usage may actually be old; you may be encountering for the first time what others encountered long ago. You can find out which is the case, of course, by looking in a dictionary or two.

2. Advertisers are not the best guides for those of us who want to write with precision. They sometimes reject the careful

writer's grammatical usage—see **LIKE, AS.** They sometimes take pains to tell us that their enunciation is folksy: *fish 'n' chips.* And they often coax the unwary to stretch a word beyond its boundaries.

Take *album,* for example. The core meaning of *album* is a book of blank leaves, pockets, or envelopes for storing photographs, stamps, phonograph records, and so on. In the days when phonograph records revolved at 78 revolutions per minute, that was the only meaning of *album.* When a piece of music ran to multiple discs, they were sold in *albums.* Then the "long-playing" discs (33-⅓ rpm) came on the market. One of them held as much music as an entire album of the old discs. The advertisers cried, "A whole album on one record!" Nowadays, of course, *album* in its overstretched sense means no more than a long-playing record or disc.

The transition from *market* to *supermarket* to *mini-mart* is another example. For still another, see *house* and *home* under **EUPHEMISMS** 2.

Since precision is rarely the interest of advertisers, it is no surprise to find that sometimes they themselves only vaguely understand their "messages." For example, a local supermarket was advertising "everyday low prices." RHD says that *everyday* means (1) daily, (2) of or for ordinary days, as contrasted with special occasions, and (3) ordinary, commonplace. We asked the assistant manager what he meant by "everyday low prices."

He answered, "Well, we put special low prices on certain items every Tuesday and every weekend."

So he didn't mean low prices every day; that is, *daily.* We wondered whether possibly he meant *commonplace* or like those all over town, so we asked, "But what do you mean by *everyday?"*

"Well, it's the company's slogan."

"Yes, we can see that," we said, "but what does the slogan mean by *everyday?"*

"Well, uh, gee, I don't know what it means."

Some people argue that a word takes on whatever meaning writers choose to give it. In the long run, that is true. The difficulty is to know whether the long run has arrived. When you encounter a word with which you are not familiar, or one used in a sense with which you are not familiar, how can you tell whether *your* readers will understand the word in the sense that you understand it? The easiest way is to look in a dictionary.

If you question a writer's use of *cohort* in place of *companion*, dictionaries will tell you that the usage is widespread, regardless of the fact that the older and still standard mean ing of *cohort* is *group*. Many readers will understand if you use *cohort* to mean *companion*, especially if your context is clear, although many careful writers eschew that usage. See **COHORT.**

On the other hand, you will now and then find a writer using *mitigate* to mean *militate*, a mistake few readers will accept as a shift in usage. Instead of supposing that the word has taken on the other meaning, they will snicker. See **MILITATE, MITIGATE.**

If you find a writer, or even several writers, using a word in a way that is new to you, it is risky to conclude that readers will take the same meaning you did if you use the word in the new way. Those writers may not have consulted their dictionaries. You should consult yours.

3. New words and usages crop up in the special varieties of a language more often than in the generally used main body of the language. They appear in occupational and scientific jargon (*complex, interface*), in local slang (*blizzard* was once slang), or as regionalisms. Some of the words or usages move gradually into general usage, and some don't.

When you become aware of a new word or usage, the chances are fair that you are hearing or reading something that may be common only to your occupation or your locality.

If you want to use the new thing in writing for a wider audience, look in a dictionary first. See **AUDIENCES.**

Because new usages appear in one variety of usage before they spread (if they do) to other varieties, you cannot keep up to the minute with changes in "the language." You can keep up to the minute only with some subgroup of users. If you do, you will then sound strange to other users. You must choose the group to which you prefer to sound strange. The advantage of general usage is that it sounds good enough to almost everybody. Its disadvantage is that it cannot achieve technical precision without being cumbersome and wordy. See **VARIETIES OF USAGE.**

Zinsser warns us that words that spring into the language overnight may leave it as abruptly. He reminds us that we heard frequently of *happenings* during the late 1960s, but no more, and that *"out of sight* is out of sight." Nicely, succinctly, and with flair, Zinsser says: "Be vigilant, therefore, about instant change. The writer who cares about usage must always know the quick from the dead" (p. 45).

4. Now that we have disposed of the two notions we mentioned at the outset, let us turn to the matter of dealing with new uses for old words. Some new uses, when they become widespread, effectively deny us the earlier uses. Others don't.

Since writers too often use *positive* to mean *favorable*, it has become very difficult to frame sentences so that readers will understand that we mean *without doubt*. Readers who have formed a habit of expecting *positive* to mean *favorable* will take it that way whether you intend it or not. But to accept the new usage carelessly will also miscommunicate. Writers who persistently use a word in only one of its meanings, even though it has many, often become careless about providing a context to point the reader to the particular meaning they intend. Audiences who customarily use the word in more than one sense will then wonder which of the word's meanings to take. But if you write the context to make unmistakably clear the meaning you intend for *positive*, then you no longer need the word itself. In sum, if a word becomes overused in one of its senses, the safest thing to do is to shy away from it—use some synonym—until the word becomes less popular. See **POSITIVE, NEGATIVE;** also **OVERUSED WORDS.**

When too many writers have used *shambles* to mean merely something disordered or messed up, we can no longer count on the word to communicate a scene of bloody carnage. If we want to communicate well, it does no good to use the word "correctly" and sit back smugly. Because some readers will interpret the word one way and some another, it is better to use a synonym. See **SHAMBLES.**

But some words remain useful in their earlier sense even though they become overused. For example, though many writers fall into using *this* as their only relative pronoun, forgetting about *that,* we can still make our writing more clear by using both. Readers still understand *that* because of its other senses and will quickly grasp our meaning if we consistently use *this* to point to what we are now saying or are about to say, and *that* to point to what we said earlier. See **THIS, THAT.**

Similarly, even though many writers confuse *can* and *may,* we can better keep readers straight about what we mean if we use the two words consistently in their core meanings. See **CAN, MAY.**

Whether you feel an urge to persist in an old usage or to relinquish it, you might want to pause to think whether doing the one or the other will help clarity or hinder it.

5. We occasionally encounter the argument whether changes in usage impoverish or enrich the language, or perhaps neither or both. In the long run, of course, we don't have to worry. Just as it has always done, the language will change and it will serve. The pains of change are those of the short run—

the usages by others to which you and we must adapt. If the oldest of us complain the most, it is because we have had to adapt the most.

6. Some claim that without widely followed rules, no one can write with precision. Others counter that people are always inventing new ways of making images with language, often precisely through breaking the rules. Both are right.

Language serves both rationality and intuition, both precision and poetry. Here, in pidgin English, is a description of a schooner with three masts and two stacks over an auxiliary engine, in all a much larger vessel than the canoe of the Polynesian speaker: "Three piecee bamboo, two pieces puff-puff. Walk along inside, no can see."

That is hardly objectively precise. Masts of schooners are not made of bamboo. Puff-puff is about as vague a description of an engine with stacks as one can find. Walk-along-inside-no-can-see gives an equally vague picture of hull construction. As a guide to building another three-masted schooner with an auxiliary engine, the Pidgin description is hopeless. But as a picture of the meeting of two cultures, it is superb. Full sentences, a technical vocabulary, standard grammar, and precise syntax could describe the same meeting only at twenty times the length, and at the end the sparkle, the essentiality, and the sadness would be gone. For more on precision, see **DEFINITIONS** 5 and **PRECISION.**

CHART: See **TABLE, FIGURE, CHART, EXHIBIT.**

CITING: It is customary in scholarly writing to cite the work of other authors. Some writers may do so just to show how many books they have read, but there is also a more serious reason: to tell readers where they can get more information on the topic you are writing about. You might cite another author to show readers that you are not the only one holding an opinion you have stated—that someone else agrees with you. You might cite a source of empirical data to back up a factual statement you have made. You might cite a review of literature that can round out the readers' appreciation of the scope of a topic. You might point readers to a more detailed discussion of a topic you merely touch on. You might point readers to a mathematical derivation of a formula you use, and so on.

Many writers, unfortunately, leave us guessing. Some readers will want to pursue further information of a certain kind, but they cannot decide whether to pursue it until they know the kind of information that is in the article or book the author has cited. Here is an actual example of the kind of citation that infuriates us:

> She drew on their respect to maintain control, sometimes in directive ways, sometimes in ways that drew out and developed the controls from within (Redl and Wineman, 1952) the children.

Why should we get Redl and Wineman off the library shelf? What information will we find in the book? Do Redl and Wineman tell how to draw out and develop controls from within? Do they give the theory about controls from within? Do they contrast directive ways and drawing-out ways? Did they invent the phrase "controls from within"— is the author of the sentence merely giving credit to Redl and Wineman? Or do they perhaps tell more about that particular teacher? Or about similar teachers? We may be interested in one of those questions and not others. We cannot judge whether to go to the trouble of getting the book from the library unless we know to what kind of further information the author is pointing us.

No reader is going to dig up every reference cited on the chance that it might be interesting. If you hope your readers will care enough about your subject that they will want to read more about it, do them the courtesy of telling them the kind of information they can find. Here are some ways you might do it:

> Redl and Wineman (1952, pp. 263—75) describe in detail the method of drawing out controls from within.
>
> . . . (the phrase is from Redl and Wineman, 1952, p. 17).
>
> For another example, see Redl and Wineman (1952, pp. 78—84).
>
> Redl and Wineman (1952) review the literature.
>
> (Redl and Wineman, 1952, Chapter 7, give empirical data.)
>
> Redl and Wineman (1952, p. 19) make the same point.

Notice that we included page numbers in our examples. It is maddening to be told that there is a valuable piece of information somewhere in a 600-page book.

Give in to your self-regard. Take it for granted that at least some of your readers will be captivated by what you write and will *want* to know more about it. Then be considerate of them: tell them the kind of information they will find and the page they will find it on.

Finally, some citations are superfluous. It seems to us unnecessary to give credit for an assertion that readers of social science have long taken as true or for words that might be spoken by any of us, scholar or not, any day of the week. Here are three examples:

> Individuals vary in their degree of openness to learning and using new experiences (Alderfer, 1976; Rokeach, 1960).
>
> Aristotle was one of the greatest of the ancient philosophers (Jones, 1978).
>
> In the words of Mark Smith and Claude Johns (1968), "Where is policy formulated and who makes it?"

CLAUSES, RESTRICTIVE AND NONRESTRICTIVE: See **COMMA** 6.

CLUE, CUE: A *clue* gives you an idea about the solution of a problem or mystery. A *cue* is a reminder, a prompting, or a signal to start an action. "That remark of the chairperson was a clue to what had been going wrong between the committee and us; we also took it as our cue to leave."

COHORT: Originally, a *cohort* was a division of a Roman legion. That meaning has been extended to any group, band, or company of persons. Until recently, it was rarely used to mean an individual member of a group, band, or company. Now RHD and Webster III give *companion* or *associate* as one of the standard meanings of *cohort*. But 69 percent of AHD's usage panel find that usage unacceptable. See **USAGE PANELS.**

COLLECTIVE NOUNS: See **PLURALS** 2.

COLON: Fowler says the colon "has acquired a special function: that of delivering the goods that have been invoiced in the preceding words"—as in his own sentence. It is often handy instead of *namely, that is, to wit,* and the like.

COMMAS
   1. **Open punctuation** is the practice of leaving out commas where custom, meticulously followed, would put them in. For example, "In the fall we went to Chicago." It is customary, or at least never wrong, to put a comma after an introductory prepositional phrase such as *In the fall.* But in that example, since the sentence reads with no ambiguity and with no awkwardness of rhythm, the comma is optional.
   Here is another example: "During the course of the work we undertook special activities to strengthen the effectiveness of the research team were instituted." There, *were instituted* comes as a surprise; the reader must go back and hunt for the place the comma should have been put (after *undertook*), so the comma is not optional.

Try this one: "The decision to change is made by top management sometimes with but often without input from personnel who might be affected by the change." That sentence could have been composed by a teacher of writing as an exercise in punctuation. As a matter of fact, it comes from a book on conflict in organizations. Make it instead: "The decision to change is made by top management—sometimes with, but often without input from personnel who might be affected by the change." But it would be even better to rewrite, shifting to active voice and removing a bit of jargon as we go: "Top management makes the decision to change. It sometimes uses ideas from those who might be affected, but often it does not."

2. **Series.** Should there be a comma after *white* in *red, white, and blue?* Judging from the books, articles, and manuscripts we have read, a sizable minority of writers believe there should not be. But APA, Baker, Bernstein, the Chicago Manual, Copperud, the Ebbitts, Fowler, the Morrises, Strunk and White, the style manual in the *Second College Edition* of AHD, the "Handbook of Style" in *Webster's New Collegiate Dictionary*, the *Style Manual of the American Institute of Physics* (Hathwell and Metzner, 1978), and the *Style Manual* of the U.S. Government Printing Office (1973) all say to put it in.

Some sentences with more than one noun in each of the elements of the series would be impossible without the final comma. For example: "The engineers divided the work week into three periods: Monday and Tuesday, Wednesday and Thursday, and Friday and Saturday."

If you use Latin abbreviations with the word *et* in them, remember that it means *and*, and punctuate accordingly. Write *Johnson, Jones, et al.,* but not *Johnson, et al.* But see **LATIN.**

3. **Don't split off the verb.** You wouldn't write "Johnson, welcomed our new colleague." You wouldn't split off the subject *Johnson* from the verb *welcomed.* You wouldn't write "Johnson welcomed, our new colleague." You wouldn't split

off the verb from the rest of the predicate, *our new colleague.* No matter how many words are in the sentence, nor how complicated it is, don't split off the main verb from another part of the sentence.

Here are examples of the kinds of sentences that tempt some writers to put in wrong commas. The wrong commas are included: "The thing we all thought we had to put before everything else, was the . . ." And, "The thing we all thought we had to put before everything else was, the . . ."

The author of a proposal to a federal funding agency yielded to temptation in the following sentence and included an incorrect comma after *this.* "One reason for this, is to develop, within the local organization, commitment and energy for training."

Here is another example, with an incorrect comma after *curriculum:*

> The authors establish that students who are in classrooms that are led by teachers who encourage student participation in the definition of the class curriculum, do better academically than students who are in classrooms where this sort of influence is not extended to students by teachers.

No doubt the author was trying to make a complicated sentence more understandable, but the comma merely makes a bad matter worse. The sentence is afflicted by **WORDINESS** (which see); it should have been written something like this:

> The authors found that when teachers encouraged students to participate in shaping the curriculum, the students did better academically than when teachers did not do that.

4. **Parenthetical expressions.** In the following sentence, the phrase *as part of the process* is a parenthetical expression not vital to the sentence. It adds interesting information, but the sentence would carry its essential meaning without it: "The interviewer should design as part of the process a method of . . ." If you like open punctuation, you will omit

the commas. If you want to use commas, use *two*: "The interviewer should design, as part of the process, a method of . . ." If you use either of the commas alone, you will be guilty of splitting the verb from its predicate.

Many parenthetical expressions need the commas. Here is a sentence Bernstein (under "Punctuation") uses to illustrate the need for commas: "The Democrats, say the Republicans, are sure to win the next election." The same sentence without the commas does *not* contain a parenthetical expression: The Democrats say the Republicans are sure to win the next election."

5. **Before conjunctions.** When you write a sentence that is really two complete sentences joined by a conjunction such as *and, but, for, or, nor, yet, though, still, while,* put a comma before the conjunction. Think of the comma and the conjunction together as equivalent to a period or a semicolon. Write any of these:

He wanted to do it. He did it.
He wanted to do it; he did it.
He wanted to do it, and he did it.
He wanted to do it. And he did it.

When the second part of the sentence is not a complete sentence, but uses the subject from the first part of the sentence, as in "He wanted to do it and did it," do not put in the comma.

"He wanted to do it and he did it," without the comma, is acceptable because it is very simple and very short. Open punctuation in that sentence causes no confusion. In longer sentences, however, put in the commas. It is a better rule to put the comma in habitually, leaving it out only by deliberate design, than the other way around.

Here is a sentence from a proposal that must have made the day's work harder for the recipient:

For each implementation plan developed, in Kansas, the State Facilitator will communicate with the selected Developer/Demonstrator, and provide information regarding the local implementating agency.

Omit the comma after *Developer/Demonstrator.* The portion of the sentence after *and* contains no subject of its own; it could not stand as a sentence by itself. The sentence also contains other irritations that slow reading. Remove the comma after *developed;* the words *in Kansas* are not parenthetical. Substitute *implementing* for *implementating.* And see also **VIRGULE.**

6. **Nonrestrictive clauses and phrases.** Both restrictive and nonrestrictive clauses tell more about some noun in the sentence. "I was eager to see the participants who were to arrive at two o'clock." *Who were to arrive at two o'clock* tells more about the participants. But the clause can mean two different things. Were all the participants to arrive at two o'clock, none at any other time? If so, the clause adds incidental information that could be dropped without harming the main thought. "I was eager to see the participants." A clause having incidental, supplementary meaning is called *nonrestrictive;* it does not put limiting conditions on the main parts of the sentence.

Or were different groups of participants to arrive at different times? In that case, the clause is vital to the meaning of the main part of the sentence. It is then a *restrictive* clause, because it restricts the application of the eagerness to those participants due to arrive at two o'clock.

If a clause can be discarded without hurting the main part of the sentence—if it is nonrestrictive—we break it out with a comma (or with two commas if it lies in the middle of the sentence). If I mean that I was eager to see all the participants but incidentally add the information that they were to arrive at two o'clock, I write with a comma: "I was eager to see the participants, who were to arrive at two o'clock." But if

I mean that the participants I was eager to see were those due to arrive at two o'clock, I write without the comma: "I was eager to see the participants who were to arrive at two o'clock."

The misuse of the comma to show restriction or nonrestriction occurs in a great deal of scholarly and technical writing. What is more, when one goes back over a sentence to decipher it, one often finds that the meaning as written is absurd or downright ludicrous. Here are some examples. We did not invent them.

> Our job as social psychologists should be to link our theories to variables used in other disciplines, which turn out to be more fundamental than our own variables.

Presumably, the author of that sentence meant that if there are variables in other disciplines more fundamental than some of those common in social psychology, then social psychologists ought to encompass them in their theories. By his use of the comma, however, the author gave us the incidental information that (all) the variables in other disciplines are more fundamental than those in social psychology. With that comma, the author was almost saying that social psychologists should give up their own variables entirely.

Now an example from a philanthropic foundation:

> Faculty are invited to nominate outstanding colleagues, who have a primary interest in teaching undergraduates, for appointment as Danforth Associates.

That gives us the incidental information that outstanding colleagues (all) have a primary interest in teaching undergraduates, a sentiment with which many university faculty would surely disagree.

> It is not valid to aggregate the responses of different subjects, whose concepts and criteria of success may vary greatly.

That says it is not valid to aggregate the responses of different subjects. The comma leads us to think that the authors do not mean to limit the meaning of the first part of the sentence. They seem to be telling us that there is no collectivity of subjects from which responses can be validly aggregated, thus invalidating about 90 percent of social science at one stroke. Omit the comma.

> The first type of operation on information inputs to the nervous system, for which there is a need, is selection of relevant inputs for further processing.

There the author gives us the incidental information that we need our nervous systems. Somehow we suspected that all along. Finally, an example from a newspaper:

> The typical female, who had a legal abortion in 1975, was described in the report as "young, white, and unmarried."

The report, according to the newspaper, said that the typical female was not only young, white, and unmarried, but also had a legal abortion in 1975. Omit the commas after *female* and *1975*.

We have given above some examples of restrictive and nonrestrictive *clauses.* The same principles apply to phrases and words. *The senior researcher Johnson* is one of several senior researchers; we tell which by giving her name. *The senior researcher, Johnson,* is the only senior researcher, and we are giving her name as added information. Here is an example of a nonrestrictive phrase, wrongly punctuated:

> The two things that can be monitored are behavior and outputs that result from behavior as observed by March and Simon.

The second thing that can be monitored, in other words, is the output that results from behavior as March and Simon observe it. We don't think the author meant that only March and Simon are capable of observing output. We think the author meant that March and Simon said it first. Put a comma between *behavior* and *as*.

7. **That and which.** Use *that* at the beginning of restrictive clauses: "We awaited the truck *that* would arrive at noon; it would bring the food." Use *which* with a nonrestrictive clause: "We awaited the food-truck, which would arrive at noon." See **THAT, WHICH.**

8. Some writers believe that a good guide to using commas is to put one wherever one would naturally take a breath when reading aloud, but how do we allow for authors and readers who breathe differently?

We have not discussed all complications that can arise when using commas, but the points above seem nowadays to cause the most trouble.

COMPRISE: You can use *comprise* either going or coming: "The questionnaire comprised four parts" or "Four parts comprised the questionnaire." Usage leans toward making *comprise* go in the same direction as *include*. In strict usage, AHD says, "The Union comprises 50 states." But AHD says that *comprise* is increasingly used in both ways. Thirty-nine percent of its usage panel (see **USAGE PANELS**) approve "Fifty states comprise the Union," and 47 percent approve "The Union is comprised of 50 states." But *comprise* and *include* are not synonymous. Use *comprise* when you are stating all the parts. Use *include* when you leave some parts unmentioned. "The group included five Patagonians" implies that there were others from other places.

Compose and *constitute* go in the other direction. "Four parts composed (or constituted) the questionnaire."

CONCEPT: A *concept* is a mental image, idea, design, fancy, notion, plan, or the like. It can be put into words, drawings, mathematics, music, or other symbols transmissible to others.

I can symbolize my vision of a horse with the word *horse*, and that word arouses a similar concept (of a horse) in your mind. The concept is not the horse. The concept is not the word *horse*, either; that word is the symbol I use in the hope of arousing in your mind a concept similar to the one in mine. Architects form concepts of buildings in their minds. They symbolize them in drawings on paper. The builders translate those symbols into actions that erect the buildings. See also **DEFINITIONS.**

Some writers regularly use *concept* in place of *idea, plan,* or other common synonym. Perhaps they want to be dignified; see **PUFFERY** 1 and 3. Other writers use *concept* to mean the thing instead of the idea—they use it to mean the horse instead of the idea of the horse. Here is an example from a school's bulletin for parents:

> Our school's learning program is designed to enhance the concept of an open-ended learning program.

The author meant, we think, that the school's learning program enhanced open-endedness. We are not sure what open-endedness means, but presumably one could see some real, tangible behavior in the school that the author terms open-endedness. The author was claiming that the learning program enhanced that behavior. The author would not have been satisfied, we think, to claim only that the learning program enhanced people's ideas, notions, images about open-endedness without any counterpart in action. It would have been more clear to write something like: "Our school's learning program fosters open-endedness" or even "Our school's learning program is open-ended." See also **WORDINESS** 1.

The next example is from a letter to members of a professional organization:

> We look forward to seeing you in Boston. Thank you again for your support of the Regional Conference concept.

We do not think the writers were thanking the recipients for helping to shape a common image of regional conferences. Most of them had no part in designing them or organizing them. We think the writers were thanking the recipients only for signing up to attend. "Supporting a concept" is too fancy a phrasing for signing up to attend.

CONCERN: A matter *concerns* me if I am interested in it, involved in it, connected to it. I need not be worried about it to have a concern about it. But *concern* is also properly used in some contexts to convey *worry*. Be careful that your context tells whether you mean a worried or an unworried concern. See also **OVERUSED WORDS.**

CONNOTATIONS: All of us have our own personal connotations for words. As the Ebbitts say, "For one student, *school* has connotations of confinement, for another intellectual excitement, for still another sociability." A writer can do little about personal connotations.

But a writer can take into account the connotations a word gets from its several meanings. For readers who know more than one meaning of a word, the other meanings will color to some extent the meaning a writer wants to convey with it. *Intrigue*, for example, has two general meanings. One is to interest, attract, or fascinate. The other is to use underhandedness, deceitful stratagems, skulduggery. If you write "Behind the scenes, intriguing things were going on," some readers will take one meaning, and others the other. Even if your context makes it clear that you mean merely something interesting, readers who know both meanings will be ready to discover something underhanded in the interesting things behind the scenes.

Visitation is another good example. Dictionaries list its meanings something like this: (1) the visit of the Virgin Mary to her cousin Elizabeth, (2) the appearance or coming of a supernatural influence or spirit, (3) an affliction or punishment, as from God, (4) an unpleasant experience or event considered as occurring by divine dispensation, (5) a visit to make an official examination or inspection, (6) the act of visiting. *Visitation* is also often used nowadays as an honorific term when speaking about visiting dignitaries: "Next Thursday, we'll be receiving a visitation from Dr. Snodgrass." We sometimes suppress a smile at the possibility of an affliction or punishment as from God.

When you use a word having two or more meanings, it is well to keep in mind that some readers will think first of one meaning, some of another. Sometimes context can make clear the meaning you intend. At other times, Dr. Snodgrass might prefer that you use a different word.

For other words with multiple meanings that can spill over one into another, see **BURGEON, PRESENTING, PROBLEMATIC, SYSTEM,** and **THEORY.**

CONSISTENT: Dictionaries tell us that *consistent* is used to mean agreeing, compatible, congruous, consonant, harmonious, logical, repeated, even congenial or sympathetic. For many readers of scientific and technical papers, however, *consistent* is likely to have a strong connotation of the meaning that mathematicians and logicians give to the word; namely, not self-contradictory. That is, if an argument says in one place that A is greater than B and in another place that B is greater than A, then the argument is *inconsistent.*

Statements that are inconsistent in one context can be consistent in another. If A follows B on a straight line, it would be inconsistent to say that also that B follows A. But in a circle, both can be true: eight o'clock follows two o'clock, and two o'clock follows eight o'clock.

One of the basic rules of logic—Aristotelian logic, at any rate—illustrates the basic meaning. The rule is called the Law of the Excluded Middle: a thing (a concept) is either A or not-A; it cannot be both at the same time or something in the middle. To say that a thing is both A and not-A is an *inconsistency* not permitted in logic. (That is not to say that the rule applies to real things; we often say, "Well, it is and it isn't.")

Sometimes writers call a relation *inconsistent* that logicians call *intransitive*. As the earth rotates, for example, San Francisco follows London, London follows Bombay, and Bombay follows San Francisco. Since there is not logical contradiction there, logicians would call the relation *intransitive*, not *inconsistent*.

We are not urging writers to give up the common meanings of *consistent*. We are saying only that it is well to be aware while writing technical discourse that some readers may think of the logical meaning when they see the word *consistent*, and care with context will keep things clear.

CONTACT: Some people object to the use of *contact* to mean *communicate with, get in touch with, look up, find, reach, meet, call, write, visit,* or *phone*. Others don't. Baker says not to use *contact* that way, but to use one of those other words or phrases instead. Strunk and White say that, too. The Ebbitts say the usage is "more acceptable in non-business contexts than it was a generation ago, though it remains rare in formal usage." Sixty-six percent of AHD's usage panel find the usage *not* acceptable in formal contexts, and so do 65 percent of the Morrises' usage panel (see **USAGE PANELS**). Follett says the usage "is as natural to the American of thirty as it is grotesque to the American of sixty, for whom the idea of *surfaces touching* is the essence of *contact*." Bernstein says, in somewhat reluctant phrasing, that there is much to be said for *contact* as a verb. Copperud is in favor of the usage, although he notes that it "has not fully emerged into the sunshine of full acceptance." RHD says "there is no justification of the criticism commonly heard." Webster III says to go ahead and *contact* anyone you want. Whatever your preference, in brief, you will find an expert or two at your side. See also **VARIETIES OF USAGE** 1.

CONTINUAL, CONTINUOUS: The dictionaries say that *continual* is more often used to indicate intermittent action, and *continuous* to indicate uninterrupted action or space. The dictionaries also say that writers sometimes use either word for either meaning. The upshot is that if the distinction is important in what you are writing, it will be well not to let the whole meaning hang on the one word.

Continuous has a precise meaning in mathematics; in a continuous space, every two points have a third between them. See **CONTINUUM.**

CONTINUUM is used frequently by social scientists. It comes to us from physicists and mathematicians, to whom it means a space with no breaks or seams. In mathematical terms, it means a set of elements between any two of which there is a third. A continuum can be of any dimensionality. Physicists deal with the four-dimensional continuum.

Social scientists sometimes use *continuum* as if it were necessarily unidimensional: "Scores ranged from a low of 6 to a high of 78 on the aggressiveness continuum." And some apply the term to an array of points that is not continuous: "We used a continuum with five points."

If you want to respect the usage of the physicists and mathematicians, you can use the term *dimension* to mean a unidimensional array of points without specifying their closeness or spacing. The word *scale* points to the metric characteristics of a dimension, but it is nearly synonymous with *dimension* until you specify the *kind* of scale you are writing about. The word *scale* would have served as well as *continuum* in both the examples above, and better for those readers aware of the four-dimensional continuum.

See also **DIMENSION.**

COPE: To some, *cope* has a flavor of struggling frantically, hanging on by the fingernails, and so on. But dictionaries do not tell us that. AHD's definition is typical: "To contend or strive, especially on even terms or with success."

Cope is usually followed by *with* and a noun: *to cope with a threat.* Some writers follow the word with nothing: *He couldn't cope.* Seventy percent of the Morrises' usage panel do not approve of the latter usage in writing, nor do 75 percent of AHD's usage panel. See **USAGE PANELS.**

CRITERIA is the plural of *criterion.*

CRITIQUE has come to be used in place of *criticism* (see **EUPHEMISMS**). Some writers also use *critique* in place of criticize: "We critique Johnson's work with certain assumptions in mind." Neither AHD nor RHD lists *critique* as a verb. Ninety-three percent of the Morrises' usage panel would not use it as a verb in writing (see **USAGE PANELS**). Webster III, sad to say, lists *critique* as a verb.

CUE, CLUE: See **CLUE, CUE.**

CURRICULUM VITAE is the full Latin phrase that means *résumé.* Informally, it is often shortened to *vita.*

DANGLERS

1. Sometimes we leave part of a sentence dangling; we fail to arrange grammar and syntax to show how the dangling part belongs with the rest: "Having stayed up all night, the conversation was hard for him to follow." According to that

syntax, the conversation had stayed up all night. We know that's not reasonable, and we must pause a moment to think how to connect the first phrase to the rest of the sentence. The awkward structure snags attention and interrupts the flow of meaning from writer to reader.

Some sentences with dangling parts are ludicrous. Here is an example from Bernstein about George Washington's clothes: "Although sixty-one years old when he wore the original suit, his waist was only thirty-five." And from Strunk and White: "Being in a dilapidated condition, I was able to buy the house very cheap."

Many danglers are idiomatic and cause us no trouble. When we read "Interestingly, he made no answer," we have no trouble understanding that the interest arises with the author, who thought the lack of answer surprising. We do not stop to wonder how the person in the sentence managed to withhold his answer in an interesting way. We let many other idiomatic words and phrases dangle, and clarity rarely suffers: *generally speaking, getting down to brass tacks, given that, granting, judging by, more importantly, significantly, speaking of,* and (at least for those inured to them) *thankfully* and *hopefully.*

When danglers are not idiomatic, they become snags for the attentive reader to stumble over. They take the reader's mind off what the author wants to say. "After turning on the recording machine, the subjects' fingers left their every motion on our graph paper." The careful reader must stop and wonder whether the subjects or the experimenter turned on the recording machine.

Words and phrases containing no subject can easily become danglers, and they will if the reader cannot immediately find the subject. The natural place to put it is right after the subjectless word or phrase: "After turning on the recording machine, we captured every motion of the subjects' fingers on our graph paper."

2. Many of the danglers used nowadays begin with *based on*. Here is an example from a science news-magazine:

> Based on the unreleased ACS meeting paper, the public health department of the state of California will begin immediately to measure arsenic levels.

Surely, the public health department of the state of California is not based on the paper presented at the ACS. It may be based on an act of the legislature; it may be based in Sacramento; but it is not based on the ACS paper. As in many such instances, the sentence would have had no snag if it had begun *On the basis of.*

Here is another actual example:

> Residualized Academic Rank appears to be reflecting something *other* than self-concept based on its validity coefficients with the Sears subscales of .17, .07, and −.07.

That sentence says that self-concept, when it is based on (when it arises from) its validity coefficients with the Sears subscales (a nonsensical concept of self-concept, indeed), is not something that residualized Academic Rank appears to be reflecting (assessing). What the author meant was that residualized Academic Rank appears, on the basis of (judging by) its validity coefficients with the Sears subscales, to be reflecting something other than self-concept.

> We believe there's a new conservative mood in the country, based on the election.

That sentence says that the country's conservative mood is due to the election, the very opposite of what we think the author meant. Here is a more subtle example:

> A book committee was established to systematically order texts based on teacher recommendations.

But it was not the texts that were based on the teachers' recommendations (the texts were written before the committee was established), but the ordering of them. Make it: to order texts *on the basis of* teachers' recommendations.

The form *based on* modifies a noun: "a book based on a folk tale" or "the purchasing was based on teachers' preferences." The form *on the basis of* modifies a verb: "We are judging on the basis of the evidence" or "They will order on the basis of teachers' preferences."

The "based on" dangler usually appears in this form: *Based on the information at hand, I recommend* . . . Instead of *based on*, try *on the basis of, judging from,* or *using.* Alternatively, recast the sentence: "The information at hand leads me to recommend" or "My recommendations, based on the information at hand, are . . ."

In sum, look out for a dangler when you use a phrase that has no subject in it. If you use it, put the thing it refers to right next to it.

For more ways to confuse readers, see **WHAT'S THAT AGAIN?** See also **BASIS, BRING WORDS TOGETHER THAT ACT TOGETHER, HYPHENS,** and **NOUNS AS ADJECTIVES.**

DATA: Write *data are,* not *data is.* It is true that more than one dictionary tells us that general usage permits *data is,* and the Morrises' panel is split on the matter. But the technical guidebooks are adamant. The Council of Biology Editors (1978) says that *data* is plural and *datum* singular. APA says to write *data are.* The singular *datum* is in regular use in several fields of engineering. For a use of *datum* in social science, see Runkel and McGrath (1972, pp. 193—94 and 250—53).

DECIMATE: If a group of soldiers in the ancient Roman army became disobedient, the group was sometimes punished by killing a tenth of the men. The Latin word for that gave us *decimate.* For centuries, the word has meant to kill or destroy a large fraction of a group of living creatures. But it is sometimes used now to mean merely destroy or chop up. That last usage is rejected by 86 percent of the Morrises' usage panel. See **USAGE PANELS.**

DEFINITIONS: Define your terms! Well, yes and no.

1. Definition means somewhat different things in different contexts. RHD gives these several meanings for *define* (we are not quoting every word here):

> to state or set forth the meaning of a word, phrase, etc.
> to explain the essential qualities of; to describe
> to fix the boundaries or extent of
> to make clear the outline or form of
> to specify distinctly.

Two ideas run through those five meanings. One is the common idea of "telling what you mean": "You know, one of those trucks with a big thing that angles up and down and a person stands in a sort of bucket at the end, at the top, and changes the light bulbs in the street lights?" Such a definition may not be elegant, but it does the job. The other idea is that of distinguishing some things from other things— drawing a circle that puts everything you want inside and everything you don't want outside. The first meaning is closer to general, everyday discourse. The second is more formal and calls for stricter logic.

2. Logicians are stricter than the lexicographers. Dictionaries report the way people do use words. The definitions in dictionaries are *reportive* or *lexical.* But if we want to use a word in a way the dictionary does not report, we can always tell our readers, "I am going to use the word *inside* to mean . . ." That kind of definition is called *stipulative.* Some authors specify a few subtypes. See, for example, Copi (1968, p. 96 ff.), the Ebbitts, and Munson (1976, p. 99 ff.).

A common technique in defining is to specify a general class familiar to readers and then to tell the characteristics of the thing you are defining that separate that thing from the other members of the class: "*A horse is an animal that . . .*" "*By aggression, I mean any act that . . .*" You can often help the reader, too, by telling what you are *not* including: "*I do not mean to include . . .*" That tells what is outside, as well as inside, the circle you are drawing.

3. But many logicians are careful to say that definitions, strictly speaking, do not apply to tangible, empirical things, but only to *words:*

> Definitions are *not* appropriate for the things that words refer to, name, describe, characterize, or whatever. Thus we define the word "table" and not the object from which we ate breakfast [Munson, 1976, p. 99].

> definitions are always of symbols, for only symbols have meanings for definitions to explain. We can define the word "chair," since it has a meaning; but although we can sit on it, paint it, burn it, or describe it, we cannot define a chair itself, for a chair is an article of furniture, not a symbol which has a meaning for us to explain [Copi, 1968, pp. 96—97].

In logic and mathematics, a definition of a term is a string of words that specifies what the term is going to be used to stand for. Logical definitions are always stipulative. And logical definitions, since they deal only with conceptual things, can always stipulate exhaustively and exclusively the things the new term will label. For example, here is a logical definition of a *relation* on a set of elements:

A *relation on a set B* is a set of ordered pairs (b, b') of elements of B.

That definition specifies every possibility unequivocally. Everything conforming to the right-hand side of the definition (following "is") is a relation on a set. Any set of ordered pairs drawn from the set B is a relation on that set. Anything that fails to conform in any way fails to be a relation on a set. No set not consisting entirely of ordered pairs, for example, qualifies. No set not drawing its pairs entirely from within the single set B qualifies. But that exact specification can be done only with conceptual elements, not with descriptions of empirical things.

The dictionaries tell readers how most speakers of English use a word—or how most of some segment of them do. The logicians tell readers how they choose to use a word. Lexicographers tell us about agreement they have observed in the past. Logicians invite our agreement for the duration of their exposition. Neither the lexicographers nor the logicians claim that their definitions tell us what anything "really is."

4. Many "definitions" go beyond telling about the customary or stipulated use of a word and try to make a bridge with tangible reality: "I'm going to be talking about those trucks with a big thing that angles up and down and a person stands in a sort of bucket and so on. For short, I'll call those things *cherry pickers*." The writer of such a sentence wants us to let *cherry picker* stand for that long string of words, but the writer also wants *cherry picker* to come into our heads when we actually see one hoisting a man up and down. Such a guide to reality might better be called a description than a definition, but dictionaries allow it to be called a definition, and we won't quibble.

If you want to "define" or describe something in the real world, you can do it (a) by offering synonyms, (b) by enumerating or naming every member of the class, (c) by giving examples and counterexamples, and (d) by specifying the class to which the thing belongs and then telling how the thing differs from the other members of that class. Sometimes you can give examples and counterexamples not in words, but by pointing to a real object or drawing a picture of it. The Ebbitts say you can flesh out a definition or description with history, comparisons, contrasts, causal analysis, and authoritative testimony.

Of the logician's definition, the lexicographer's, and the attempt to lasso the real world with words, we are not saying that one is better or more right than another. All have their uses. It may sometimes aid clarity, however, to make clear to the reader the form of definition or description you are using.

5. Scientists have their own special variety of definition: the *operational definition*. It is a sort of stipulative description. The individual researcher chooses an operation (measurement or manipulation) in the real world that she or he will take to stand for a concept. Because the researcher chooses the correspondence and asks the reader to accept it temporarily, the operational definition is stipulative. Because it makes a bridge from concept to observable reality, it is a description. See also **OPERATIONAL DEFINITION.**

6. Every definition contains either undefined terms or terms that are themselves defined in undefined terms. In our definition of a relation on a set, the terms *set, pair, element,* and *prime* (') are undefined. It is obviously impossible to write a definition without undefined terms. Indeed, logicians and mathematicians take care to tell their readers their important *undefined* terms. For example, Kerschner and Wilcox (1950) talk a lot about logic in their book *The Anatomy of Mathematics.* You might think they would define such an important term as *logic,* but they don't. At the end of their discussion of definitions (p. 16), they say, "We shall say merely that *logic is like what we do in this book."*

In contrast to the often-heard admonition to define one's terms, it is often just as important to state one's *undefined* terms, since those are the terms on which everything else rests. Indeed, Kerschner and Wilcox call the undefined terms the "language *basis."* See also **PRECISION.**

DEPENDENT AND INDEPENDENT VARIABLES: Strictly speaking, the terms *dependent variable* and *independent variable* apply only in experimental studies; that is, studies in which an investigator alters the level of one variable to see what will happen to another. For example, an experimenter may be allowed to vary the setting of the thermostat in a room full of clerical workers to discover whether they will make more errors, on the average, when the air temperature is 90 than when it is 70. In that case, we say that the error rate *depends* on the air temperature and that the error rate is the *dependent* variable. We say that air temperature, because it can be set at the will of the experimenter, is the *independent* variable.

The logic in that example is that the level of the independent variable (air temperature) causes the level of the dependent variable (error rate) because (1) the change in error rate follows soon after the change in air temperature and (2) it is beyond belief that a change in error rate could cause a change in air temperature.

Like other scientists, social scientists are very happy when they can find a variable which, when changed, causes change in another. Many social scientists, however, are reluctant to claim, after an experiment, that change in one variable "caused" change in another. One reason is no doubt their awareness of the difficulty of fending off additional, unwanted influences on the dependent variable. In our example above, the experimenter might not have been able to avoid being seen by the clerical workers. Or various supervisory members of the company, out of curiosity, might have walked through the room or poked their heads in more frequently than usual. The error rate might have gone up not because of the air temperature, but because of the clerks' nervousness under the unusual scrutiny.

Regardless of care about logic or the wish to make modest claims, the original reason for distinguishing between the independent and dependent variables was to make clear the direction of causation. The terms *independent* and *dependent* themselves maintain that strong implication of causation. Readers of reports of experiments almost always interpret *independent* as causal and *dependent* as caused.

The terms *independent* and *dependent* are often used, too, when no variable is actually under the control of the investigator. For example, an investigator might want to find out whether later-born siblings score higher (at the age of 12, say) on an intelligence test than earlier-born. The investigator would call birth order the independent variable and intelligence the dependent variable, feeling confident in making that choice because it is beyond belief that a child's intelligence at 12 years of age could be a cause of the number of siblings born earlier. The logic is that nature was acting as an experimenter's assistant, so to speak, in altering birth order so that the experimenter could observe the children's intelligence at age 12.

Beyond those usages, the terms are often pushed to studies in which causation could go in either direction. An investigator might want to find out, for example, whether females in college who plan to pursue careers in science will score higher on a test of need for achievement than females who aspire to other careers. The investigator might believe that an inner need for achievement causes females to choose careers in science, and might therefore call need for achievement the independent variable and choice of career the dependent. But many readers of that investigator's report might be ready to believe that commitment to a professional career might cause an increase in scores on tests of need for achievement. They might even be ready to believe that some still further variable, perhaps knowledge of the women's liberation movement, might cause rises in both the other variables. When it is possible for causation to go either way or both ways at the

Figure 1

The Present Situation

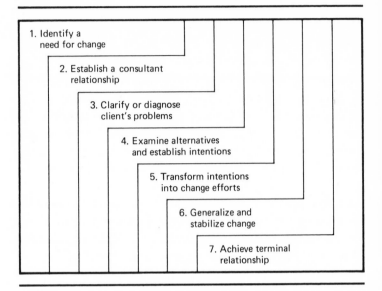

1. Identify a
   need for change

2. Establish a consultant
   relationship

3. Clarify or diagnose
   client's problems

4. Examine alternatives
   and establish intentions

5. Transform intentions
   into change efforts

6. Generalize and
   stabilize change

7. Achieve terminal
   relationship

The Desired Situation

same time, the labels *independent* and *dependent* can spark
more argument than they are worth.

DIAGRAMS: Some authors like to decorate their prose with
diagrams, regardless of whether they add any meaning to
the prose. Figure 1 is an example. The lines in Figure 1 add
no meaning; indeed, the full meaning of the diagram can be
conveyed by an introductory sentence and a list:

> The phases in moving from the present situation to the desired
> situation are (1) identify a need for change; (2) establish a
> consultant relationship, etc.

The lines in a diagram should mean something or they
are not worth drawing. Indeed, they will do harm, because

many readers will hunt for the added meaning they suppose the author intended, and they will begrudge the author their wasted effort. A line diagram will supplement the meaning in the text to the extent that its lines have obvious and precise meanings.

DIALECTIC does not mean dialogue, discourse, or discussion. It signifies a mode of reasoning and is a technical term in philosophy. Here are some of the meanings that AHD gives for it: (1) The art of arriving at the truth by disclosing the contradictions in an opponent's argument and overcoming them. (2) The Hegelian process of change whereby an ideational entity (thesis) is transformed into its opposite (antithesis) and preserved and fulfilled by it, the combination of the two being resolved in a higher form of truth (synthesis). (3) The Marxian process of change through the conflict of opposing forces. (4) Any method of argument or exposition that systematically weighs contradictory facts or ideas with a view to the resolution of their real or apparent contradictions.

DIFFERENTIAL: This word is sometimes misused as a synonym for *different,* as in *the differential mean ages of the two groups.* The word is a technical term in mathematics and mechanics. It indicates a comparison of rates—a difference of differences. A *differential* surcharge is one that varies with the amount of the base charge. The *differential gear* in an automobile enables one drive wheel to go faster than the other when the automobile rounds a curve.

Different must apply to two or more things, as *the different men.* But *differential* can apply to a single thing, as a differential surcharge or a differential gear-assembly.

"The two groups wanted different increments" would mean that the groups differed in the amount of increase they wanted. "The two groups wanted differential increments" would mean that the groups were alike in wanting increases whose amount would depend on some other condition at the time the increase was to be made.

DILEMMA is a technical term in logic denoting a choice between two equally undesirable alternatives. Dictionaries also say that using it to mean merely a problem or perplexity is standard usage. Many readers of scholarly and technical writing, however, are familiar with logical terms and rules, and they are likely to interpret *dilemma* in its technical sense. Very few of the Morrises' usage panel are logicians, if any, but 71 percent of them use *dilemma* in writing only in its technical sense. See **USAGE PANELS.**

Other words that can be used in the sense of problem or perplexity are *complication, difficulty, fix, frustration, impasse, intricacy, plight, predicament, puzzle, quandary, snag, trouble.*

DIMENSION: Physicists speak of the familiar four orthogonal *dimensions* of space-time. Social scientists, too, use the term in a technical sense, especially those who investigate problems of scaling. The technical use of the term in social science goes like this: If a property is such that every person or object has a quantity of that property that is more than, less than, or equal to that of every other person or object having that property, then that property is a *dimension.* If you use the term to mean merely a part, component, viewpoint, aspect, or circumstance (and Webster III includes that meaning as standard), you will confuse readers who think of the term in the context of physics or scaling. See also **CONTINUUM.**

DOCTORAL: Not doctorial.

DUE TO: Everyone accepts *due* used as a predicate adjective as in "The rent is due" or "The financial loss was due to mismanagement." The argument arises over using *due to* in place of *because of,* as in "The firm lost money due to mismanagement." No one seems to object to the use of *through, on account of,* or *owing to* to mean *because of,* but many writers and readers shudder at finding *due to* used that way. Bernstein, Copperud, and the Ebbitts, however, do not share the shudder. They say that not only is *due to* steadily becoming more widely used to mean *because of,* but there can be no rational objection to it. Webster III recognizes it as standard. Indeed, Fowler says the usage has become part of the Queen's English. On the other side, AHD's usage panel stands arrayed against Bernstein, Copperud, the Ebbitts, Webster III, Fowler, and the Queen: 84 percent of the panel finds *due to* unacceptable to mean *because of* (see **USAGE PANELS**). And Follett says that "the loose and lawless *due to* is still rare in writers other than those who take advantage of every latitude."

EACH, EVERY, ALL: *Each* tells the reader to put attention on the items in a collection individually, separately, one by one. Many writers nowadays seem to get *each* mixed up with *all.* For example: "We'll deal with each point one at a time" means that we'll deal with the first point one at a time, then the second point one at a time, and so on.

"The extension service has 36 field offices located in each county of the state" means that if you look in any county of the state, you will find 36 field offices in it. What the author actually meant was that there was an office in each of the 36 counties.

Another example: "Each meeting was similar." You have to consider at least two things at a time to find similarity, but the *each* tells us to consider only one meeting at a time. You can find identity doing that, but not similarity. The author meant "All the meetings were similar."

> Each year between 1907 and 1911, an average of seventy-three southern Italians repatriated for every one hundred that arrived.

Obviously, the author was talking about the number of Italians repatriated per year. But in any particular year, some particular number were repatriated; no averaging is possible with a single figure. The author meant to average over years, not within each year: "Between 1907 and 1911, an average of seventy-three southern Italians per year repatriated."

From an article about blue-green algae in Antarctica:

> Each of the lakes studied loses 2,200 to 22,000 pounds of such material per year.

It is likely that the author meant that some lakes lose less of such material per year and other lakes more, not that each of the lakes varies in its loss per year between 2,200 and 22,000 pounds. We think the author meant "The lakes studied differ in their annual loss of such material, the losses ranging from 2,200 pounds to 22,000 pounds."

Every also points to separate items, but it puts more emphasis on every one of them being counted. *Each person spoke out* implies that the persons spoke one at a time, but we are not entirely sure that every last person at the meeting spoke. *Every person spoke out* tells us that no person was silent, but we are not entirely sure that the persons spoke one at a time. *All spoke out* makes it entirely possible that several were speaking at once. Literally, *all* means every last one, but when all spoke out, the silence of one or two may have gone unnoticed.

We read this sentence in a book review: "Each of the book's chapters is of high quality." Since the author wanted to point out the uniformly high quality of the chapters, *every* or *all* would have been smoother. Another example involving similarity:

> The most fundamental similarity between the Soviet system and capitalism is the primacy each places upon economic growth.

Make it: *the primacy both place.*

Some inept uses of *each* become patently absurd: "Can each of the three roles be brought together?" Make it: *Can the three* or *Can all three.* Another absurdity: "Each chair was of the same design." Make it: *All the chairs were.* Another: "Each person was gathered in the same room." Another: "the intersection between each of the two components."

ELEGANT VARIATION: The label is Fowler's. Bernstein calls it *monologophobia* and says that writers who suffer from it have a "compulsion to call a spade successively a *garden implement* and an *earth-turning tool.*"

Injecting synonyms can be distracting even when you write for a general audience. Injecting them into technical writing can cause serious confusion. For example, you might write a series of sentences or paragraphs describing questionnaires with which you and your colleagues assessed certain variables: *We constructed the X questionnaire by . . . We put together the Y scale by . . . We compiled the Z measure by . . .* Readers of technical articles often read very carefully to learn what things you did similarly and what things differently. The changing words *constructed, put together,* and *compiled* may lead them to think you did things differently that you actually did similarly. And *questionnaire, scale,* and *measure* are of course technical terms. The reader who encounters different technical terms in succession will immediately look for an explanation. If you do not want the reader to look for differences, choose a word and repeat it: *We constructed the X questionnaire by . . . We constructed the Y questionnaire by . . . We constructed the Z questionnaire by . . .* See also **PARALLELISM.**

Here are two examples from Fowler's long list—which he gives, he says, "to nauseate by accumulation of instances":

> The export trade of the U.S. with the Philippines has increased by nearly *50 percent,* while that of the U.K. has decreased by *one-half.*

Dr. Tulloch was for a time *Dr. Boyd's* assistant, and knew *the popular preacher* very intimately, and the picture he gives of *the genial essayist* is a very engaging one.

EUPHEMISMS

1. Euphemisms don't last long. Inevitably, they take on the meanings of the words they replace, and still further euphemisms must then be found—if we insist on using euphemisms.

Some time ago, many educators became aware that many audiences were being bored by *lectures*. They now give *presentations*. Are the audiences less bored? See **PRESENTING**.

Critics are often harsh in their *criticism*. Since we don't want to frighten people with the threat of adverse criticism, we offer them a *critique* instead. Are the recipients less anxious? See **CRITIQUE**.

A place for defecation and urination was once known as the *jakes*—from the French *Jacques*. When that word acquired a bad odor, the English borrowed again from the French and began using the euphemism *toilet*, which originally meant cleaning and grooming. When that no longer fooled people, they turned to *bathroom*. But everyone knows what people do in a bathroom, and we keep hunting for fresh euphemisms: *lavatory, restroom, men's* or *women's room*, and *john*—and with the last we come almost full circle.

The word *undertaker* has a lugubrious sound. Do undertakers think *mortician* and *funeral director* do not? The United States once had a *War Department*. Perhaps people here or abroad believe we have given up belligerent attitudes now that we have a *Department of Defense*.

At the time the Eighteenth Amendment to the Constitution of the United States was ratified, millions of people wanted to do away with the harm done by the alcohol obtainable in *saloons*. Care was taken not to bring back saloons after the repeal of the Eighteenth Amendment. We have *taverns, bars,* and *cocktail lounges* instead.

We used to call old people *old.* Now we call them *elderly* or *senior citizens.* Do the oldsters feel younger? Few people seem to want to be *janitors,* but many people seem to think they don't mind being *custodians.* Bulletins from the nuclear power industry have described a fire as an incident of *rapid oxidation* and explosion as an *energetic disassembly.*

2. Strictly speaking, a euphemism replaces a word generally considered blunt, harsh, and unpleasant: *pass away* for *die, defense* for *war, assaulted* for *raped,* and even *rapid oxidation* for *fire.* But the same word-magic is often used on words signifying nothing unpleasant in the hope of making a pleasantness even more pleasant.

Home for *house* is an example. Edgar A. Guest once wrote: "It takes a heap o' livin' / In a house t' make it home." Not any more it doesn't. All it takes is listing by a real estate agent. Only a few decades ago, a *house* was a structure, and a *home* was, as RHD nicely puts it, the place where "one's domestic affections are centered." But the real estate agents wanted us to think we were buying affection along with the structure. Inexplicably, their customers imitated their usage, and nowadays *home* means no more than *house* to most people. To convey the earlier meaning, we must now go to the trouble to say something like "I want to have a place where I can settle down, become a part of the community, and be glad to come back to after I've been away." Now that the real estate agents have worn the magic off *home,* to what word can they turn?

Perhaps the use of *positive* to mean *good* or *favorable* came about because of a wish to sound scientific. See **POSITIVE, NEGATIVE;** also **GOOD.**

The technique of euphemism can even be worked in reverse. People rich as Croesus have been known to say that they have enough money "to maintain a certain standard of comfort."

Presumably, their intent is to avoid stirring up envy and resentment. This reverse technique pretends that something is *less* desirable than most people think it to be.

The reversed euphemism seems to have overtaken social scientists' use of the word *theory*. Many, judging from their circumlocutions, seem to believe it immodest to apply the word to their own work. See **THEORY**. See also **GENDER, PUFFERY,** and *visitation* under **CONNOTATIONS**.

EVERY: See **EACH, EVERY, ALL.**

EXHIBIT: See **TABLE, FIGURE, CHART, EXHIBIT.**

EXOTIC: Years ago, *exotic* meant little more than being foreign, from another country. Now, however, it is widely accpeted in every variety of usage to mean strikingly unusual or beautiful. Webster III adds all these connotations: *strange, mysterious, romantic, picturesque, glamorous, rich, showy, elaborate,* and *pertaining to strip-teasing.* The current array of meanings prevented us from being sure of the author's meaning when we encountered this phrase: *evidence generated by exotic statistical and computational techniques.*

FEEDBACK: See **POSITIVE AND NEGATIVE FEEDBACK.**

FEEL: See **BELIEVE, FEEL, THINK.**

FEWER, LESS: Apply *fewer* to things that can be counted separately, such as apples, people, words, and so on: "Fewer people attended, and they brought less enthusiasm." Use *less* for things that do not break naturally into countable units: enthusiasm, water, confidence, energy, sunshine, and so on. Write *fewer expressions of enthusiasm* and *less enthusiam, fewer quarts* and *less water, fewer calories* and *less energy, fewer foot-*

candles and *less sunshine, fewer grains* and *less sand, fewer pebbles* and *less gravel, fewer kernels* and *less corn,* and *he has fewer years left* but *he is less than 60 years old.* Eighty-five percent of the Morrises' usage panel maintain the distinction we make here. Seventy-seven percent of AHD's panel prefer *fewer people* to *less people.* See **USAGE PANELS.** See also **MAJOR, MAJORITY.**

FIGURE: See **TABLE, FIGURE, CHART, EXHIBIT.**

FINALIZE: Eighty-six percent of the Morrises' usage panel refrain from using *finalize* in writing (see **USAGE PANELS**). Try *complete, conclude, finish.*

FIRSTLY, FIRST OF ALL: Fowler says that insisting on *first* instead of *firstly* is as much a "harmless pedantry" as the converse. Other writers on usage insist on *first.* You might write *firstly* and *secondly,* but would you write *seventhly* or *thirteenthly?* See also **IMPORTANT.**

First of all instead of simply *first* is redundant. *Second of all* and *third of all* are sheer verbosity.

FIRST PERSON: The misapprehension persists among academic writers and graduate students that editors frown upon the use of the first person, especially the first person singular. If you leaf through some articles and books by social scientists, however, you will find that a good portion of them are written in the first person. Only once have we had an editor complain about the first person singular in one of our manuscripts, and he accepted it anyway. APA, the Council of Biology Editors (1978), and the *Style Manual* of the American Institute of Physics (Hathwell and Metzner, 1978) all approve of the first person singular.

It is true that some writers and editors still believe that investigators should pretend to be disembodied—that they should write, for example, *It was decided that . . .* , as if a decision forms itself somewhere outside a human brain. If you prefer to be disembodied, go ahead and write that way. But see **ACTIVE AND PASSIVE VOICE.**

FORTUITOUS, FORTUNATE: An event is *fortuitous* if it happens by accident or chance. It is *fortunate* if you are glad it happened. If you read "It was fortuitous that more Republicans showed up than Democrats," you should not conclude that the writer is a Republican.

FUNCTION: For many social scientists, perhaps most, *function* means about the same thing as *relation*. For mathematicians, *function* has a more-restricted meaning: a relation in which, for any value of the variable x, there is exactly one value of the variable y. For mathematicians, a regression line plots a function; a correlation does not. When you are reporting an analysis of data in which the shape of a relation is important, you might want to be careful about *function*.

GENDER: Some careful writers in the social sciences have recently been using *gender* to mean the social role attached to being one sex or the other. If writers were careful, *gender* could become a recognizable synonym for *sex role*. Unfortunately, many writers are not careful, but seem to be using *gender* merely as if it were a new "in" word for *sex*, as in "The subjects were grouped by gender."

Writers who wish to distinguish between *gender* and *sex* must, of course, use *both* words, choosing carefully their application of each.

GENERAL SYSTEMS: See **SYSTEM.**

GLEAN: The core meaning of *glean* is to gather grain left behind by reapers. By extension, it has come to mean picking up something bit by bit, as to pick up bits of information through meticulous perusal. Lately, usage has extended even further to merely finding out, learning, ascertaining, or discovering. For many readers, however, glean retains the flavor of getting something little by little or slowly.

GOOD is an ancient and honorable word still in approved use in respectable circles. If you want to say that something is good, *good* is just as first class as *positive* and less subject to multiple interpretations. Similar remarks apply to *bad* and *negative*.

Some scientific writers wouldn't want to be caught dead saying that anything is good or bad. Wanting, nevertheless, to get across the idea that they find some things desirable or undesirable, some apparently use *positive* and *negative* as euphemisms, hoping not to be accused of making judgments of value or of having a personal feeling in the matter. But the camouflage on euphemisms wears thin quickly, and it has already worn through on *positive* and *negative.*

We have our own guess about the new widespread use of *positive* for *good* and *negative* for *bad.* We think it came about because of the increases in the proportions of young people attending college and enrolling in social science courses. When we were undergraduates, no one used *positive* to mean *good.* But our professors in social science were even then using *positive* to distinguish one direction of behavior from another. Of course, they all revealed, sooner or later, the directions in which they wanted people to change, and they all, we noticed, labeled their preferred directions with *positive* instead of *negative.* We think many students, then and since, paid close attention not only to their professors' vocabularies, but also to their preferences about behavioral change and concluded, however wrongly at times, that they should say and write *positive* instead of *good* when they wanted to sound scientific. If our hypothesis approaches the truth, it would not be the first time a technical term has been watered down in general usage.

A bit of evidence that using *positive* for *good* is a recent usage appears in the 1947 edition of Funk and Wagnalls' *Standard Handbook of Synonyms, Antonyms, and Prepositions.* Although that book lists 73 synonyms for *good, positive* is not among them. See also **EUPHEMISMS** and **POSITIVE, NEGATIVE.**

GOT, GOTTEN: Use either.

GRANT, PROPOSAL: A *proposal* is a document asking for a *grant* of money. Sometimes people speak of "writing a grant." They mean writing a *proposal* or writing *for* a grant. They get the *grant* when the money arrives.

GROUND ZERO is sometimes used as if it meant a starting point, as in "We had to go back to ground zero." The phrase comes from ballistics; it means the point intended to be exactly under the explosion of a bomb or projectile. The correct analogy is a target or intended end-point, not a starting point. Here is a correct (if overblown) use of the analogy: "Everything was ready and at last we were over ground zero. We dropped our information on the chairperson. and it had the effect we expected."

HOLISTIC: *Holism* is a philosophical term denoting the theory that whole entities have an existence other than as the mere sum of their parts. Also spelled *wholism*. Don't write *holistically* if you mean merely *as a whole*. See **PUFFERY.**

HOMOGENEOUS, HOMOGENOUS: *Homogeneous* means having parts all of the same kind. *Homogenous* is a technical term used in biology to indicate a correspondence in structure due to common origin. If you use *homogenous* to mean having parts that are alike, some readers will think you don't know how to spell *homogeneous,* and readers familiar with the biological use of *homogenous* will be confused.

HOMOPHILY: This word has been appearing here and there in the literature of social science to refer to resemblance or similarity due to common ancestry or social background. We cannot find *homophily* in any dictionary. (If we could find it, surely it would mean love of sameness.) We do find *homophyly,* for which dictionaries give the meaning in which writers are using *homophily.* We think users of *homophily* should be spelling it *homophyly.*

HOPEFULLY: "Hopefully, he rang the doorbell." That used to mean that he was hopeful as he rang the doorbell. Now it seems to mean that I hope he rang it. Technically, the new usage dangles (see **DANGLERS**), and some of us find it annoying. We cannot, it is true, argue our case on grammar. English carries several danglers that are idiomatic: *interestingly, generally speaking,* and others. But if we cannot discourage writers from using *hopefully* to mean *I hope* by arguing grammar, we can at least warn them that the usage will turn away some choleric readers. Seventy-six percent of the Morrises' usage panel will be among them (see **USAGE PANELS**). And APA (p. 40) says:

> *Incorrect:* Hopefully, this is not the case.
> *Correct:* I hope this is not the case.

HOWEVER: Some words signal the reader that the writer is changing the direction of thought: *but, therefore, however,* *nevertheless, conversely, though,* and others. Most of these signaling words can go gracefully almost anyplace in a sentence. *But* and *provided that,* however, are impossible to put at the end, and *but* and *nevertheless* are especially strong at the beginning.

However, especially, should be placed carefully. It seems to work most smoothly, drawing attention to the change of direction instead of to itself, when it is put neither at the beginning nor at the end, but inside, as near the beginning as is reasonable—as we did in the last sentence of the previous paragraph.

Zinsser, in his chapter 13, says that *however* at the beginning of a sentence "hangs there like a wet dishrag" and at the end "has lost its 'howeverness.' "

HUMAN: *Humankind* is as good a compound as *mankind* and less sexist. And since *human* is now widely accepted as a noun (if not by Follett), it can be used in place of *man,* as in "Humans can talk" instead of "Man can talk." See also **SEXIST LANGUAGE.**

HUMANISM: A few decades ago, *humanism* was a word used chiefly by scholars to name the growth of the individualistic and critical spirit during the European Renaissance; that is, the growing attention to the capabilities of humans in their own right and the lessening attention to the religious scheme of things. Erasmus was probably the movement's best-known spokesman. Now, *humanism* has come to stand for another change of attention, this time away from humans as stimulus-response mechanisms but toward the same concern for human initiative, values, and dignity. Follett prefers that we not use *humanism* to mean *humaneness, humanity,* or *humanitarianism.*

HYPHENS: Many writers nowadays seem to have given up hyphens. Perhaps they hope to avoid putting a hyphen in the wrong place by not putting one anyplace. It is true that there are no simple rules. Bernstein says, "The world of the hyphen is anarchic." The Chicago Manual, unable to enunciate any simple rule, gives several pages of detailed examples. Nevertheless, an author can get into as much trouble without hyphens as with them.

1. Hyphens are especially needed when several words come before a noun as adjectives and especially when one or more of those words are themselves nouns. Without trying to state a rule, we give some examples to illustrate the ease with which ambiguity creeps in where hyphens are absent.

What are *two day trips?* Two trips made during the day— *two day-trips*—or trips of two days each—*two-day trips?*

What are *two age cohorts?* Cohorts containing two ages— *two-age cohorts?*—or two cohorts distinguished by age—*two age-cohorts?*

What is a *teacher counselor?* A counselor of teachers, or a teacher who is also a counselor? If the latter, the meaning is clearer with the hyphen: *teacher-counselor.*

Is a *one year old alternative school* an alternative school that is one year old—*one-year-old alternative school?* Or one of several alternative schools, each a year old—*one year-old alternative school?* Or an old alternative school offering a one-year curriculum—*one-year old alternative school?*

Some time ago, we read an account of a study that ran over several years. The investigators made two extended visits to the field each year, one visit longer than the other by design. Their total time in the field was greater in the first year than in any later year. At one place in their report, they spoke of *the first year long phase.* Did they mean the first year, thinking of each year as a phase—*the first year-long phase?* Did they mean the longer of the visits during the first year—*the first-year long phase?* (Better, of course, would be *the long phase in the first year.*) Did they mean the period of field work in the first year, which was longer than later yearly periods—*the long first-year phase?* We couldn't tell.

Often, of course, the reader can work out the meaning from context. But the point is that the reader should not be asked to stop and work it out. Use appropriate hyphens or recast the sentence.

2. Hyphens do not serve well to connect phrases. The reader's eye goes first to the two words the hyphen lies between; the reader tries first to make sense of that coupling. Here is a good example: *self-reference group similarity.* The author of that phrase meant similarity between self and reference group. He tried to indicate the idea of *between* with the hyphen, only to produce a commonly hyphenated compound: *self-reference.* Somehow, neither the author nor the journal editor was able to see the garble.

Here is a sentence from a newspaper:

> The shortfalls are the result of a continuing trend: the failure of revenues from sources such as building permits, engineering fees, and other non-property tax revenues to keep up with inflation.

The writer obviously had in mind fees from building permits, engineering fees, and other revenue that does not come from property taxes. Unfortunately, the writer tried to connect *non* to *property tax* with a single hyphen. But the hyphen between *non* and *property* does not succeed in bringing together *property* and *tax.* Instead of reading on, we must stop and wonder whether the writer thinks that building permits and engineering fees are tax revenues.

Another example: the *Oregon Junior High-Middle School Association.* To us, that sounds like a junior association for high-middle schools, whatever they might be. Presumably the people who thought up that name spoke of *junior highs* and *middle schools* dozens of times a day, came to think of the phrases as single words, and thought they could make a compound of them with a hyphen. Authors who suppose that all their readers speak the same jargon they themselves speak are bound to confuse many of their readers, incur their derision, or discourage them from reading further.

Here is another monstrosity: *University of Chicago-Illinois State University.* See also **VIRGULE.**

3. When you put the compound adjective after the noun, you do not need the hyphen:

two-day trips, but trips of *two days.*

One *year-old* alternative school, but one alternative school a *year old.*

In-depth data collection, but data collection *in depth.*

A *fast-sailing* ship, but a ship *sailing fast.*

An *in-service* workshop for teachers, but a workshop for teachers *in service.*

On-site work, but work *on site.*

4. Some strings of letters can be used either as separate words or as prefixes. *Over* is a separate word in "They disagreed over intensifying the treatment" but a prefix in "They were over-intensifying the treatment." When using a word as a prefix, either make it solid, as in *overcompensate, overspend, underestimate, underpay,* and *backfire,* or hyphenate it, as in *under-fund, under-represent, under-load, back-formation, full-fledged,* and *full-scale.*

5. Always hyphenate when you make a compound with *self: self-referral, self-confident, self-esteem,* and the like.

6. When you use a hyphen in typescript, it is customary to type it without a space on either side.

APA has two useful pages (pp. 55–57) on hyphens. The Chicago Manual has helpful comments on pages 162–164 and a long and helpful table of examples on pages 176–181. The *Style Manual* of the U.S. Government Printing Office (1973) offers everything but the kitchen sink on pages 73–130. And Copperud is very good on hyphens. See also **NOUNS AS ADJECTIVES.**

IDENTIFY: The core meaning of *identify* is to verify the identity of something: to identify a fly as *Musca domestica*, to identify the person coming down the street as your spouse, to identify the handwriting as George's, to identify an idea as Amy's. Freud added another meaning: to perceive one's own identity as merging with that of another person or group.

Lately, *identify* has been appearing in the sense of *choose* or *designate*, as in "Three persons were identified to lead the three groups" or "We identified three aspects of the problem for special attention." That meaning does not appear in AHD, RHD, or Webster III. See **OVERUSED WORDS** for alternatives.

The strangest use of *identify* we have found was its use to mean *calculate:* "The range and median for the schools reporting a change were identified." We find it perplexing that so many writers seize upon *identify* when good, serviceable words like *choose*, *designate*, and *calculate* are available. Do those writers like to sound scientific, and do they picture an entomologist in a white coat identifying *Musca domestica?* See **PUFFERY** and **OVERUSED WORDS.**

IMPACT: "A vast crowd impacted St. Peter's Square." RHD says this does not mean that the crowd collided with St. Peter's Square, but that it congested the square. AHD, RHD, and Webster III all agree that *impact* is used as a noun, as in speaking of the impact of one thing on another. They also agree that it is used as a verb meaning to press firmly into something, to pack in, to congest. That's as far as AHD goes. RHD and Webster III, however, say that *impact* is also being used to mean strike, collide with, or have an impact, as in "When the speaker flashed the last picture on the screen, the full meaning of his proposal impacted the audience." Many readers and writers find that usage distasteful.

IMPLY, INFER: If you get these two mixed up, your readers won't infer correctly what you hoped to imply.

IMPORTANT: "The group voted to do it. What was more important, the vote was unanimous." It is idiomatic, in such a sentence, to drop *What was* and simply write "More important, the vote was unanimous." Some writers make it *More importantly.* Seventy-five percent of the Morrises' usage panel make it *More important.* See **USAGE PANELS.** For an analogy, see **FIRSTLY.** See also **DANGLERS.**

IMPUGN, IMPUTE: To *impugn* is to attack, assail, call into question: "She impugned the chairperson's motives, accusing him of duplicity." To *impute* is to attribute or ascribe: "She imputed duplicity to him."

INDICATE comes from the Latin *index*, or forefinger. In all its current usages, *indicate* retains that core meaning of pointing. In its extended usage, it means something other than your finger that points or signifies, as in "His grinding teeth indicated his emotion." The meaning is even extended to using words, but few enough words that they serve more to point than to explain: "She said enough to indicate her reluctance, but not enough so that I could decide what to do." Synonyms for the last meaning are *suggest, intimate,* and *hint.*

Scholarly and technical writers have frequent occasions to mention the writings of others. Many writers seem to have two favorite words for doing that: *indicate* and *suggest.* For example: "Johnson indicates that the recent rise in delinquency is leveling off." "Johnson has suggested that factor analysis could illuminate this problem." Both examples stretch *indicate* and *suggest* beyond their limits. *Indicate* and *suggest* are synonyms for *point, signal, intimate,* or *hint,* not for *say, write, report,* or *claim.* See *indicate* under **OVERUSED WORDS.**

INFINITIVE, SPLIT: Splitting an infinitive is not a sin, but neither is it a grace. When an infinitive makes trouble, it is usually best to rewrite the sentence. Here is an example: *the failure of researchers to commonly define intrinsic motivation.* If we try to unsplit the infinitive in that sentence, we get into trouble in both directions, with the *failure of researchers commonly to define intrinsic motivation* and with *the failure of researchers to define intrinsic motivation commonly.* All three versions make the reader stop and think about what is meant. But the author could have written *the failure of researchers to use a common definition of intrinsic motivation.*

Here, from a university bulletin, are two simple examples: *to better serve the candidates* sounds better to our ears written *to serve the candidates better; to periodically travel* sounds better as *to travel periodically.*

INPUT: Neither AHD nor Webster III lists *input* as a verb. That is, they do not include as standard usage a sentence like this: "Several people inputted their ideas into early drafts." RHD lists the verb only in its use in computer technology: "The next step is to input the data into memory."

In all three dictionaries, the heavy emphasis in all meanings is on machinery and computers. One makes inputs of energy into a machine, information into a computer. It is a long extension from those meanings to making "input" to a design for an experiment, a conversation, or an early version of an article for a journal. Such a use of *input* will seem overextended to many readers. For alternatives, see under **OVERUSED WORDS.**

INROAD: An *inroad* is a hostile invasion, raid, incursion, encroachment. It is not merely an entry, opening ploy, or interjection.

IN-SERVICE: When using *in-service* as an adjective in front of a noun, don't forget to put in the hyphen. See also **HYPHENS** 3.

No dictionary says that a noticeable number of people use *in-service* as a verb. Do not *in-service* your people.

INTERFACE: The core meaning of *interface* is a region or system that serves as a junction between other regions or systems. And the activity going on in the interface is different from the activities on either side, although it depends on them. The interface between sea and air is a world of surface tension different from the sea below or the air above, although it exists only because of both. The interface between two computers makes translations neither computer makes alone, but it can make them only because of the inputs and outputs between itself and the computers.

AHD, RHD, and Webster's *New Collegiate Dictionary* give very similar meanings for *interface*. They run more or less like this:

> A surface forming a common boundary between adjacent regions.
> The device or system by which interaction is effected.
> The place at which independent systems meet and act on or communicate with each other.

Interface first came into use in the physical sciences and then in computing technology. When we move the metaphor to the social sciences, we can reasonably call a liaison committee an interface, and on the same logic so can we a traveling salesman. Despite the small smile the second example may bring, both the committee and the salesman do carry on the special function of connecting other systems that distinguishes an interface. But if we describe a conversation between two people as *interfacing*, we eviscerate the term.

If the special qualities of the interfacing function are indeed what you are writing about, by all means use the technical term. But if you are writing about people, conversations, conferences, and committee meetings as all of us understand them, don't show off with *interface*. Use the common words.

IN TERMS OF

1. This phrase seems to be irresistible to the verbose writer. When you find *in terms of* two or three times on a page, you almost always find that the page could be a third shorter. We give here several sentences from such pages, following each with a shorter or clearer rewriting.

> The group discussed how the project could be sustained in terms of replication with limited resources. [Instead use: The group discussed how the project could be replicated with limited resources.]

> procedures found to be effective in terms of the participative planning process. [Instead: procedures found to be effective in participatory planning.]

> conceptualizing organizations in terms of boundary maintaining systems. [Instead: conceptualizing organizations as boundary-maintaining systems.]

> The attitudes of teachers were very negative in terms of students. [Teachers had very unfavorable attitudes toward students.]

> Johnson could be a good resource person in terms of day-to-day contacts. [Johnson's resources could be used well in day-to-day contacts.]

> In general, the type of institution appears to be relatively unimportant in terms of the programmatic characteristics which we investigated. [Programs differed little among types of institutions.]

2. Properly used, *in terms of* tells the reader that you are pointing to a certain kind of *term*. When you write "Let us put that in terms of mathematics," you are saying that you now want to use the kinds of terms mathematicians use: numbers, letters, and operators. You can, however, simply write "Let us put that into mathematics."

Here is another example of the proper use of *in terms of*:

The more clear, explicit, and firm the running of the school, the less the disruption in terms of student victimization.

That sentence characterized disruption in victimizations per student. *Victimizations* and *student* are the *terms* used to characterize disruption. Again, the sentence could be recast:

When a school is run with clear, explicit, and firm rules, fewer students are victimized.

Below are two more examples using *in terms of* properly. The terms referred to are dollars, units, and time (probably years). Although it is possible to rewrite these two examples so as to omit *in terms of*, we could not find a way to rewrite them without losing some clarity or emphasis.

Reckoning output in terms of dollars, we get . . . , but in terms of units reaching their destination, we get . . .

In terms of the time it will take to replace the property, the loss is staggering. In terms of the time it will take to replace the human community, the loss is incalculable.

See also **WORDINESS** 1.

INTRIGUE: See CONNOTATIONS.

KIND: Write *that kind of thing is*, because *kind* is singular, and so must be *that*, *thing*, and *is*. Similarly, *this kind of book contains*, and so on.

Write *those kinds of things are* when you are writing about more than one kind. Similarly, *these kinds of books all contain*.

Do not write *those kind of things are* nor *that kinds of thing is*. Nobody writes the latter, but some do write the former.

Don't think you can avoid thinking about this usage by using *those kinds of things are* for every occasion, because you will often be writing about only one *kind*, and then you must use the singular.

The same usage applies to *sort*, *class*, and any other word signifying a collectivity.

LAST NAME FIRST: It is often useful to list names in some order; the alphabetical order is a convenient one, and it is customary to alphabetize by last name instead of first or middle name. It is easy to find a surname in an alphabetical list if that name is put first. But for reasons we cannot fathom, some authors and editors insist upon putting the last name first no matter where the name appears. We like the way the American Sociological Association and the Ebbitts enter names into references or bibliography. They treat names of multiple authors like this: Johnson, A. B., C. D. Johnson, and E. F. Johnson.

LATIN: Although scholars gave up writing in Latin some centuries ago, most still use some Latin abbreviations. Perhaps it is a way of letting people know our status, since we no longer wear our caps and gowns on the street. We have encountered many undergraduates, however, and even some graduate students, who do not know i.e. from e.g., not to speak of op. cit., loc. cit., or sup. Indeed, we come upon confusion of *i.e.* and *e.g.* once in a while in print. Since Latin abbreviations are Greek to many readers, we recommend giving them up entirely.

Writing without Latin abbreviations is easy; you can see it done in any magazine you pick up. One of us, with a friend, wrote a scholarly text without using a single Latin abbreviation, not even et al. in the references.

You might care to have a list handy, anyway, since you will go on encountering Latin phrases and abbreviations in what you read. (Note that nowadays common Latin phrases and abbreviations are set in Roman type, not italics.) The Chicago Manual (pp. 384—88) lists 58 of them. Below are the more frequent:

> ad hoc: for this special purpose, with respect to this subject or thing. Often used to designate a temporary committee.

ad hominem: to the man. Applied in verbal contentions to mean an attack upon an opponent's character instead of an answer to the opponent's argument.
ca., *circa:* about, approximately
cf., *confer:* compare
e.g., *exempli gratia:* for example
et al., *et alii:* and other people
etc., *et cetera:* and other things or people
et seq., *et sequentes:* and the following
ibid., *ibidem:* in the same place
i.e., *id est:* that is
loc. cit., *loco citato:* in the place cited
N.B., *nota bene:* take careful note
op. cit., *opere citato:* in the work cited
q.v., *quod vide:* which see
v., *vide:* see
viz., *videlicet:* namely

And for good measure, here are two common English abbreviations:

ff.: and the following pages, verses, etc.
p. (plural pp.): page (pages)

Now and then we encounter et al. in the possessive, as in "Johnson *et al.'s* hilarious book on social relations among prairie dogs." For us, that has the same antic humor as *OH's* governor, the *Dr.'s* orders, and storming the *Ft.'s* gates.

LEARNING: In the educational literature, we often come across sentences like this: *If children are to learn, we must* . . . or *Children will learn more if the conditions* . . . Learn what? Humans (like other creatures) don't just learn; they learn *something.* They learn to read, they learn the multiplication tables, they learn how to psych out the teacher, they learn to obey, and so on. When you write about learning, you will be more clear if you state what it is that your learners are learning—or what you want them to learn.

Writers sometimes write as if humans do not learn any-thing—that they remain in a sort of stasis—unless they are in a classroom and unless they are doing what the teacher wants them to do. But humans are always, unavoidably, willy-nilly, learning *something*. If you specify what it is that your learners are learning, or might learn, you will avoid giving the impression that you think humans learn things only at the behest of others.

LESS: See **FEWER, LESS.**

LIKE: AHD and RHD both say that using *like* as a conjunction is nonstandard. That is, if you have two complete sentences that you want to connect into one, don't connect them with *like*. For example, you might have the phrases *Winston tastes good* and *A cigarette should* (taste good). You could connect them this way: "Winston tastes good, and a cigarette should" (taste good), or this way: "Winston tastes good, as a cigarette should" (taste), or several other ways. But not: "Winston tastes good, like a cigarette should." Using *like* as a conjunction is unacceptable to Follett, to more than 75 percent of AHD's usage panel, and to 88 percent of the Morrises'. See **USAGE PANELS.** Following AHD, RHD, Follett, and the Morrises, we would refrain from writing "Like I said, only three participants were older than sixty." We would write *As I said.*

Both Bernstein and Copperud give very clear and useful discussions of the use of *like* and *as.* Copperud quotes a rule set forth by Frank O. Colby: If *as, as if,* or *as though* makes sense in a sentence, *like* is incorrect. If they do not make sense, *like* is the right word.

Bernstein goes to great length, and Copperud to some length, to explain that the antipathy toward using *like* as a conjunction has no justification in the history of English nor in analogies to the use of other conjunctions like *after* and *while.* If you use *like* as a conjunction, you will have the sympathy of historians of grammar and of those who, with or without historical knowledge, like to use *like.* But those who are horrified by *like* as a conjunction are likely to be the more vocal.

LOGICAL: The core meaning of *logical* is: in accordance with logic. And the core meaning of *logic* is: the principles of reasoning, especially of the structure of propositions distinguished from their content.

But we often come upon sentences like this: "It was only logical that he would vote no" or "It was the logical form of organization for that purpose." We can expect those sentences to be acceptable to a general audience even if we do not know the sentences that went before or after them. AHD, for example, gives "reasonable on the basis of earlier statements *or events*" (emphasis ours) as one of the standard uses of *logical.*

What the writers of the examples above meant, we suppose, was that given the premises they had in mind, anyone following the rules of logic would conclude what they concluded. But readers had to take those authors' word for their logicalness; they did not set down their premises.

Social scientists and other scholars might want to be more precise in their use of *logical.* Scholarly writers claiming a statement to be a logical derivation can satisfy their readers' natural curiosity by stating the premises from which they draw the statement, just as they satisfy their readers' curiosity about the fall of numerical data by giving statistics.

But if you mean only that you were not surprised when he voted no, or that you thought the form of the organization well suited to its purpose, then use words like *appropriate, fitting, natural, proper, reasonable, sound, suitable, unsurprising.*

MAJOR, MAJORITY: You have to be able to count a *majority*. You can't count a *major* part; you just tell by bulk. Write: *a majority of the remarks* but *a major part of the discussion*. And *a majority opinion* (meaning that a majority of individuals hold it) but a *major theory* (meaning that it attracts a great deal of attention). The distinction is the same as that between *fewer* and *less.* See **FEWER, LESS.**

MALAPROPISMS: See **WHAT'S THAT AGAIN** 4.

MAN: In its sense of humankind, see **HUMAN.**

MARGIN: If 55 percent of a body votes in favor and 45 percent votes against, do not write that the measure carried by a margin of 55 to 45. *Margin,* in this sense, means the excess, what is left over, or degree of difference. Write that the vote carried by a margin of 10 percent.

MAXIMUM, MINIMUM, and other limits

"We should allow a minimum of three to five years." We wish the author of that sentence had made up his mind whether we should allow no less time than three years or no less than five. The author might have meant something like: "This kind of job ordinarily takes at least five years, although with a great deal of luck we might do it in three."

A *minimum* is a point (not a range or band of values) beneath which something should not or cannot go. If the time can go below five years to three, then five years cannot properly be called a minimum. Conversely for *maximum.*

"The mice died within two to six minutes." That sounds as if the author was not sure whether the mice died before two minutes had passed (within two minutes) or before six had passed. Actually, the author meant that the first mouse died two minutes after the precipitating event and the last six minutes after it: "The mice died between two and six minutes later."

One also encounters phrases like *at least thirty or more.* But *at least thirty* means thirty or more, and *thirty or more* means at least thirty. Enough is enough.

ME, I: *Me* is not less right or less respectable than *I.* One is right in some places, the other in others. No one needs to be told to write "*I* (not *me*) was invited to the conference" and "They invited *me* (not *I*) to the conference." The rule is the same when you have more than one object of the verb or preposition; they are all in the objective case (*me*): "They invited *her, him* and *me* (not *she, he,* and *I*)," "They invited Johnson and *me* (not *I*)," and "They wrote to Johnson and *me* (not *I*)."

Do not substitute *myself* for *me.* Write "They invited Johnson and *me*" (not *myself*). Use *myself*—and *himself, herself, themselves*—only reflexively "I assigned the job to myself" and intensively "I myself do not hold that opinion."

MEANINGFUL: Few words in English are less meaningful than *meaningful.* Here is a typical example: "Recent theorizing makes the study of the neocortex particularly meaningful." Readers will naturally assume that theorizing about the neocortex has some meaning, even a particular meaning. Would the author be mentioning the matter if it did not have? If the author had immediately gone on to tell the particular meaning he had in mind and for whom, some meaning would have been put on *meaningful.* But he didn't.

But you can avoid all that. You can simply tell the meaning you have in mind without the preliminary *meaningful.* Consider this sentence, for example:

> Children in many families lack meaningful relationships; they remain alienated from the adult world, from their peers, and from themselves.

There the author did go right on to tell what she meant by *meaningful relationships.* But the author could have dropped those words without losing any meaning:

> Children in many families remain alienated from the adult world, from their peers, and from themselves.

For alternatives to *meaningful,* see **OVERUSED WORDS.** See also **WORDINESS.**

MEDIA: *Media* is plural; *medium* singular. A newspaper is a *medium* of communication; the press, the radio, and the ballet are *media.*

METHODOLOGY: *Methodology* and *method* have come to mean pretty much the same thing. In strict analogy with some other words ending in *-ology, methodology* ought to mean the *study* of method, or the principles used in thinking about or choosing methods, and that is what it often means in colleges of education. But aside from that special meaning, it is hard to see much difference in the relevant meanings given in dictionaries for the two words. When you are writing about a way of doing something, *method* will do as well as *methodology.* See **PUFFERY.**

MINUSCULE means very small. It is cognate with *minus,* not with *miniature.* Spell it with two *u's.*

MODEL: The core meaning of *model* is that of a small version of the real thing: a model railroad, a model of the Empire State Building, or a plastic model of the human body with its organs. A model shows in small scale how the real thing works at full scale. To check on how their designs will work, engineers often build a model before they begin on an actual dam, power plant, or canal. Not far from that meaning of *model* is another: something to be emulated. A fashion model shows how you will look (presumably) if you wear the same clothes.

You can use *model* with strongest effect if you save it for one of those two meanings. It is weaker when you use it to mean analogy, chart, delineation, depiction, design, diagram, image, interpretation, line of action, map, outline, plan, plot, procedure, proposal, representation, routine, scheme, sequence, or theory. See also **OVERUSED WORDS** and **THEORY**.

MYSELF: See **ME, I,** and **USAGE PANELS.**

MYSTERY, MYSTERIOUS, MYSTICAL, MYSTIC, MYSTICISM: A *mystery* is something secret or unknown, something obscure or puzzling, or even just something arousing curiosity or speculation. And something *mysterious* has the character of a *mystery*. So far so good.

But *mystery* has another sort of meaning, too: a truth unknowable except by divine revelation. The adjective for that meaning is *mystic* or *mystical*: spiritually significant or symbolic, pertaining to the supernatural, or pertaining to *mystics* or *mysticism*. And *mysticism*, in turn, is the doctrine of an immediate spiritual intuition of truths transcending ordinary understanding. The noun *mystic*, not surprisingly, means one who gives credence to the doctrine of mysticism.

The two families of meaning obviously touch each other, but they are obviously different, too. If you use *mystic* or *mystical* to mean merely *mysterious*, you will confuse readers who are aware of the spiritual denotations of *mystic* and *mystical*. See **CONNOTATIONS.**

MYTH has two meanings. One is any fictitious, unproved, or even erroneous belief or idea, probably the meaning most often encountered in general usage. The other meaning, an ancient one, is a story or character type that embodies cultural ideals or stirs commonly felt emotions. In the second meaning, the story or character type can be true, untrue, or partly true. In that sense, Eisenhower was as much a myth as Paul Bunyan. The second meaning of *myth* is an important technical term for anthropologists and other social scientists.

NOUNS AND VERBS: Baker, Follett, and others inveigh against using nouns to carry the bulk of one's meaning. Writing moves with more vigor when the verbs carry their share. In the following examples from Follett, the phrases at the left put the bulk of the meaning in the noun, little or none in the verb. The verbs at the right carry the meaning themselves.

apply pressure	press
give authorization	permit, authorize
send a communication	write
take appropriate action	act
lose altitude	descend, drop, come down

Sentences stuffed with nouns move on elephants' feet. Here is an example of galumphing nouns:

> Stage I was the review of the literature. Stage II consisted of the revision of the questionnaire, the development of the Memorandum of Agreement, and the acquisition of the names and addresses of potential respondents. Stage III was the meeting with Abernethy and the consequent revision of the Memorandum.

And here we have replaced several nouns with verbs:

> In Stage I we reviewed the literature. In Stage II we revised the questionnaire, drafted the Memorandum of Agreement, and gathered names and addresses of potential respondents. In Stage III we met with Abernethy, afterward using his suggestions to revise the Memorandum.

Nouns sit dully, but verbs work willingly. Listen to their vigor as they work for Zinsser: "They push the sentence forward and give it momentum. Active verbs push hard; passive verbs tug fitfully."

The Council of Biology Editors (1978, p. 20) gives an example of changing nouns to verbs and the passive voice to active. Compare the following examples:

> Following termination of exposure to pigeons and resolution of the pulmonary infiltrates, there was a substantial increase in lung volume, some improvement in diffusing capacity, and partial resolution of the hypoxemia.

> After the patient stopped keeping pigeons, his pulmonary infiltrates partly resolved, lung volume greatly increased, diffusing capacity improved, and hypoxemia lessened.

NOUNS AS ADJECTIVES: Putting two names of things—two nouns—next to each other is the most primitive way to use language. If you want to say that there is some sort of connection between a man and a hat, one way to do it is simply to put the two words together: *man hat.* Of course, that does not convey a very exact meaning. You might mean a hat belonging to the man, or you might mean a hat suitable for male wear. Our language enables us to be more precise: the *man's hat* and *hats for men.*

Nothing is "wrong" in using one noun to modify another. We do it frequently in English, and more often than not we are understood well enough: ice house, brick house, economy drive, cattle drive, pupil control, worker control, and so on.

But notice how much you must know about context, how much familiarity you must have with those paired words, to interpret them correctly. An ice house is a house in which ice is stored, not a house made of ice like an igloo. With a brick house, it is just the reverse: a house made of bricks, not a house where bricks are stored. The grammatical structure won't tell you the differences in meaning; the grammatical structures are identical. You can know the difference only from having learned the meanings of the pairs as if they were single words.

We hear of things that drive the economy, such as an industry or a monetary policy. But we know that an economy drive is not one of those; it is an effort to economize. But a cattle drive is an occasion on which cattle are driven.

Pupil control and worker control may be less familiar than the other examples. If you are a teacher, you know that pupil control is the control *of* pupils, not control *by* pupils. And if you are familiar with the history of relations between labor and management, you know that worker control is control *by* workers, not control *of* workers. You must be familiar with those realms of discourse to understand the phrases.

If career education means education about careers, and moral education means education about morality, does quality education mean education about quality? No, it means education of good quality. If quality education means education well accomplished, does quality control mean control well accomplished? No, it means control of the quality of something. Again, the grammatical structure is not enough to tell us the right meaning.

When you put nouns together in clusters that are not thoroughly familiar to your readers, it is easy to fall into ambiguity. We have collected a string of examples to show how easy it is.

Are *taxpayer problems* the problems of taxpayers or perhaps problems the Internal Revenue Service is having with taxpayers?

Does *physician assistants* mean assistants to physicians or physicians who are assistants?

Is *patient satisfaction* the satisfying of patients, the satisfaction felt by patients, or satisfaction mixed with patience?

Does *teacher reports* mean reports about teachers, reports by teachers, or reports to teachers?

Is *organization behavior* the behavior of organizations, the behavior of people in them, or the behavior of organizing?

Does the *principal influence* mean the chief influence among several or the influence from a school's principal?

How about *pre-college teacher development?* Does that mean the development of teachers before they get to college? Or perhaps *pre-college teacher* is meant analogously to *3rd-grade teacher,* so that *pre-college teacher* means someone who teaches subjects or grades that are taught before the college years. When we queried a well-placed friend, we discovered that the latter meaning is understood among those versed in educationese. But lest you blame educators for this example, we should tell you that we took it from an announcement issued by the National Science Foundation.

We recently saw this book title: *Achieving Patient Compliance.* We thought at first that it was a book on how to maintain one's composure while complying with the demands of modern civilization. It turned out, however, to be a book for physicians on how to get patients to do what they are told.

On a bulletin board, we saw a notice that managed in only two words to leave us stupefied: *Vacancy Positions.*

Sometimes a string of nouns as adjectives can be readily understood, but it strains readers' patience while they wait for the final noun. One writer managed to put three nouns and two adjectives between the preposition *of* and its object *programs: the goals of the elementary and secondary education teacher preparation programs.* See **BRING WORDS TO-GETHER THAT ACT TOGETHER.**

What can you do instead of putting noun cheek by jowl with noun? You can use adjectival forms: *administrative* decision, *experimental* design, *parental* care, *assisting* physician. You can use participles: *advanced* placement, *released* time, *delayed* signal, the information *reported.* You can use the possessive: *man's* hat, *teachers'* development, *taxpayers'* problems, *patient's* satisfaction, *leader's* absence. You can use prepositions: hats *for* men, reports *from* analysts, assaults *upon* teachers, behavior *within* organizations, influence *of* the principal, control *by* workers.

ONE ON ONE: This phrase presumably comes from basketball and has connotations of one person aggressively watching and possibly obstructing another. If you want to indicate a simple matching or correspondence by pairs without the overtones of guarding, the better phrase is *one to one*, as in "We asked the participants to lay out their two kinds of marker one to one." If you use the phrase as an adjective preceding a noun, put hyphens in it: "We arranged one-to-one meetings of members of the two groups." And see **HYPHENS.**

OPEN SYSTEM appears increasingly in the literature of social science. Unfortunately, some writers treat the phrase as if no other kind of system existed. Some writers mention both *open systems* and *closed systems*, but seem to imply that there are no finer classifications to be made.

Boulding (1956) has distinguished eight levels of system: (1) A *framework* is a static system like the steel skeleton of a building. (2) A *clockwork* system has moving parts; the solar system is an example. (3) A *cybernetic* system transmits information within itself, as a thermostat does. (4) An *open system* is a self-maintaining system that depends on matter, energy, and information from its environment. Life appears at this level. (5) The *blueprint* system reproduces itself through a genetic "blueprint." Plants exemplify this level. (6) *Imaging* systems construct maps within themselves of their environment and themselves within it. Animals with brains exemplify this level. (7) *Symbol-using* systems make images of images; humans exemplify this level. (8) *Human social organizations* make use of humans as components.

Boulding's systems are nested. That is, each level of system contains the characteristics of systems lower than itself; it is distinguished from them by an *added* capability. Systems at levels 4 and above are *all* open systems, but of increasing complexity and capability.

You may not like Boulding's scheme. Our point is that among open systems, it is possible to distinguish several types. And among human systems, some of the other distinguishing features are just as important as openness to environment.

See also **SYSTEMS.**

OPERATIONAL DEFINITION: Social scientists thank the physicist Bridgman (1927) for having given them the idea of the operational definition. Bridgman said that an operational definition of a thing tells readers what they can do and what they can look for to bring it into their experience.

An operational definition of a variable can specify the operation necessary to measure it; the example is often given of defining intelligence as the number you get when you administer an intelligence test and score it. An operational definition of a variable can also specify the operations necessary to alter the variable; an example is defining reinforcement of an animal during learning by specifying how the animal is to be reinforced, or not, for specific behavior. Traditionally, the investigator selects a *single* operation as the operational definition of a particular variable in a particular study.

The operational definition gives discipline, it reminds researchers not to claim too much for their measures—not to suppose that to grasp a yardstick is to grasp an ultimate reality. But the idea of the operational definition had another, far-reaching effect on psychologists, sociologists, and other behavioral and social scientists. It forced them to pay attention, forever afterward, to the ways that different ways of measuring variables can produce very different outcomes of experiments.

One used to see every so often in the professional journals a plea for researchers to adopt a common measure of some particular variable. The yearning seemed to be like that of Archimedes when he said that if he had a lever long enough and a fulcrum to rest it on, he could move the world. Nowadays one sees those pleas less often.

Campbell and Fiske (1959) told us once and for all that there is no fulcrum from which, with one lever, we can lift into view the secrets of behavior. We cannot become more confident of the knowledge we take from our studies, they said, by insisting that every researcher choose one and the same operational definition of a variable—not even if that one measure can somehow be shown to be better than all others. The world of measurement, error, reliability, and validity they displayed is Einsteinian, not Archimedian; a measure or a variable tells us what it does only because of what other measures of that variable and of other variables also tell us. No measure has an absolute meaning; the world is relativistic.

At the same time, working in the realm of test theory, Cronbach, Rajaratnam, and Gleser (1963) were thinking similar thoughts. They are explicit in saying that the relativity of measures goes beyond traits and methods to population, situations, and even the purposes of the investigator. Their concept of generalizability includes and goes beyond reliability and validity. Indeed, not only do different kinds of testing design send generalizability in different directions, but so do different research designs.

McGrath, Martin, and Kulka (1982) have indeed pursued the same kind of thinking into research strategy. Just as there is no single best measure of a variable, there is no single best study design. And just as one measure takes its meaning from being compared with others, so one study takes its meaning from other studies of the same topic by different methods.

"Weaknesses of methods," McGrath, Martin, and Kulka say (p. 109), "are to be made explicit, so that they can be compensated for with other, complementary methods, in subsequent research. . . . Knowledge accrual requires convergence of findings derived from divergent methods."

Bridgman prodded us. And now the methodology of social science can never be as simple as it was in 1927, or even in 1959.

See also **DEFINITIONS.**

ORAL, VERBAL: *Oral* means the use of the mouth. *Written* means to be read with the eye—or in the case of Braille, with the fingers. *Verbal* includes words transmitted through any medium. *Verbal* is sometimes used as synonymous with *oral*, but if you want to be sure your readers understand that you mean spoken language, you are safer with *oral*.

Verbal always means words, and *nonverbal* always means something other than words. Though *verbal* is sometimes used to mean oral, *nonverbal* is never used to mean nonoral. It always includes grunts, screams, gestures, facial expressions, or any sort of nonword communication.

OVERSIGHT: To *oversee* is to supervise. People speaking governmentese are now using what seems to be the natural noun form of that verb, *oversight*, to mean supervision, as in *That committee has oversight of* in contexts where the use of the verb would bring *That committee oversees.*

That usage seems awkward to those of us, including AHD, for whom the core meaning of *oversight* is "an unintentional omission or mistake." It is too easy to construct sentences that verge on confusion, as in this example:

In its oversight of dam construction in the nation's rivers, the committee seems to have forgotten . . .

We recently heard a master of ceremonies get so mixed up that, when he wanted to say *overlook*, he made a new verb out of *oversight:* "In our list of people to whom we are grateful for making this occasion possible, we oversighted the stage hands."

See also **NOUNS AND VERBS.**

OVERUSED WORDS: Almost all words have synonyms—words that obviously overlap in meaning but retain their own distinctive flavors, such as *snicker, snigger, chuckle, chortle, giggle,* and *guffaw.* You overuse a word if you repeatedly use only one from a group of synonyms in places where another would convey your meaning more precisely. If many other writers use that same word in neglect of more suitable synonyms, the word becomes overused generallly. Since readers then encounter the word in many different contexts, they no longer look for a precise meaning in it. Writers, in turn, can not longer use the word to carry the more precise meaning it once had.

There are times when you want to point only vaguely. (That sentence is an example; we maintained the vagueness by using the word *point* without an object.) Words with vague meanings are useful. The danger is to fall into using vague words when you want to be precise.

Writing is hard work. All of us tire at some point and lose the alertness to be careful, specific, and precise. The temptation becomes irresistible to seize the first word that comes to mind and to dump a half-formed thought into it, still hoping to have a sentence that seems to read all right. When you catch yourself doing that, put a circle around the dump-word and return to it when you have more energy.

When a word becomes severely overused, its residual meaning falls back toward one of the primitive semantic dimensions such as the evaluative, as readers familiar with the work of the psychologist Charles Osgood and his colleagues will not be surprised to hear. Linguists have observed the process. They use the term *counterword* to describe a word so overused that little is left of its original meaning but a general flavor of approval or disapproval, as with *fine, great, nice, cute, darling, awful, terrific*. Some of the words in the list to be given later may be on the way to becoming counterwords. For another example, see **EXOTIC.**

When a word is sufficiently abused, so much of its meaning can drain away that nothing is left but a sort of verbal tic. The word *value*, for example, is used so constantly by advertisers that it loses almost all its meaning for them and can no longer stand alone. The result is oddly redundant phrases such as that used by the automobile dealer who offers *true value quality*. Isn't it enough to offer *true value* or *true quality?*

Some words are overused simply by being used where no word is necessary. *Area, process,* and *situation* are common examples. In the following sentences, nothing is lost by omitting the italicized words:

> He taught *in the* sociology *area.*
> They wrote the chapter on *the area of* the psychological aspects.
> The negotiation *process* went on for a long time.
> She carried out four experiments on *the* competition *process.*
> It was an emergency *situation.*
> Because of the quick dartings of the insects, the observation *situation* was difficult.

For some other unnecessary words and phrases, see **WORD-INESS.**

Naturally, words that seem overused (Fowler and the Morrises call them *vogue words*) to writers for newspapers and general magazines will sometimes seem necessary technical words to academic writers. Here are some *vogue words* listed by the Morrises: *input, output, hangup, watershed, overview, empathy, infrastructure, ongoing, seminal, in-depth, feedback, escalate, relevant, clout, interface, parameter, ingroup, outgroup, peer group, synergy.* Some of those words will seem indispensable to social scientists who need them for special technical meanings. But the Morrises are not complaining about the proper use of technical terms. Indeed, they would like to protect the precision of technical terms by discouraging their intrusion into general discourse as vague analogies and metaphors.

We list below some words that seem to us overused in scholarly articles and books. We are not urging that these words be entirely given up, but that others might be used where sharper meaning is wanted. Among the alternatives given for each word, you may find a word or phrase that more precisely conveys the meaning you want. Words appearing as separate entries in this book are set in capitals.

ADDRESS (as in *we must address the task*): attend to, bear in mind, carry out, deal with, direct or turn one's attention to, do something about, go toward, make plans for, orient, think about, work at.

APPROACH (as in *to get that done, our approach was to*): means, method, procedure, scheme, strategy, tack, tactic, technique, way.

APPROACH (as in *the approach we take in discussing these ideas*): assumption, conception, consideration, idea, image, impression, notion, opinion, outlook, perspective, persuasion, point of departure, sense, slant, standpoint, surmise, **THEORY,** thesis, thought, values, viewpoint.

AREA (topic or part): category, component, division, domain, kind, matter, part, piece, portion, range, realm, scope, section, sector, space, sphere, sort, subject, topic.

ATTEMPT: aim, attack, endeavor, essay, hazard, pursue, seek, strain, strive, struggle, tackle, try, venture, wrestle.

Challenge: argue with, contend, contest, debate, demand, dispute, object, oppose, quarrel, question, stimulate, summon, take exception.

Communicate: confer, consult, converse, deal with, discourse, discuss, exchange, interact, report, talk, talk over, thrash out, transact.

CONCERN (to be involved with): affect, affinity, attract notice, bearing, connected, contact, contemplate, draw attention, engage, engross, fascination, interest, link, pertain to.

CONCERN (worry): anguish, apprehension, care, disquiet, distress, dread, fear, fluster, foreboding, misgiving, perplexity, strain, tension, trouble, uneasiness, worry.

CONTACT: call, communicate with, converse with, find, get in touch with, look up, meet, reach, talk with, telephone, visit, write.

Credible (worthy of confidence): acceptable, accredited, authentic, believable, creditable, dependable, inspiring confidence, meritorious, reliable, reputable, responsible, trustworthy.

Definite (in the sense of justifiable or undoubted appropriateness, as in *they think it has a definite place* or *it is a definite addition to*): appropriate, confident, deserved, entitled, justifiable, legitimate, **POSITIVE,** proper, secure, worthy.

IDENTIFY (pick or single out): choose, cull, decide upon, designate, fix upon, list, name, pick, point to, recognize, select, single out, specify, winnow from.

IMPACT: affect, bear upon, buffet, bump, **CONCERN,** connect with, **CONTACT,** drive, encounter, give impetus to, have effect on, hit, impinge upon, influence, jolt, meet, move, pertain to, press, push, run afoul of, shock, stir up, strike, thrust, touch upon, urge.

Implement: accomplish, actualize, act upon, bring about, bring to pass, carry out, carry through, commit to action, effect, execute, fulfill, make, operate, perform, put into effect, realize, transact, work out.

INDICATE (as in *Johnson and Kreitlow indicate that*): allude to, assert, claim, describe, explain, express, imply, intimate, mention, point out, say, state, tell.

INPUT (as *to make an input to the discussion*): make a contribution; offer an idea, opinion, etc.; take part in.

INPUT (as "to input your ideas"): describe, explain, express, propose, say, set forth, state, tell.

Involve (include, join, as *the group was willing to involve him in their activities*): associate, band together, commit oneself, connect, devote oneself, embrace, engage, entail, include, join, merge.

Involve (engross, preoccupy, as *They were so involved in the task that they didn't hear the bell*): absorb, devote oneself, engage, engross, enthrall, fascinate, give attention, interest, preoccupy.

MEANINGFUL: adequate, advantageous, applicable, auspicious, effective, efficacious, efficent, eloquent, emblematic, explicit, expressive, gainful, handy, hinting, implicit, indicative, influential, meaty, momentous, pithy, portentous, potent, powerful, pregnant, prognostic, significant, suggestive (see **INDICATE**), useful, valuable, weighty.

Meet (as in "meet the needs"): acknowledge, allay, alleviate, answer, assuage, fulfill, gratify, indulge, quench, quiet, relieve, respond to, satisfy.

MODEL: guide, ideal, image, map, method, pattern, picture, plan, procedure, strategy, style, **THEORY,** view of things, way.

Negative (in the sense of lacking in constructiveness, helpfulness, optimism, cooperation, or the like): bad, burdensome, deleterious, detrimental, disadvantageous, harmful, hopeless, inappropriate, inauspicious, inconvenient, inexpedient, inopportune, painful, prejudicial, trying, undesirable, unfavorable, unfortunate, unprofitable, unsalutary, unsuitable, useless, wearisome. For words to indicate "negative" acts or feelings toward other people, see any thesaurus under *exclusion, harm, hatred, hostility,* and the like.

Ongoing: chronic, constant, continuing, evolving, going on, lingering, periodic, perpetual, persistent, progressing, recurrent, relentless, repeated, steady, unbroken, unflagging, uninterrupted, unrelenting, unremitting.

POSITIVE (in the sense of laudable, to the good, beneficial): admirable, advantageous, appropriate, auspicious, beneficial, convenient, desirable, favorable, fortunate, good, gratifying, helpful, hopeful, laudable, opportune, profitable, propitious, salutary, splendid, suitable, useful, valuable, wholesome. For words to indicate "positive" acts of feelings toward other people, see any thesaurus under *friendliness, sociality,* and the like.

Problem: block, complication, confusion, difficulty, **DILEMMA,** fix, frustration, hindrance, impasse, intricacy, obstacle, perplexity, plight, predicament, puzzle, quandary, snag, trouble.

RELATE (to other people): assist, collaborate, communicate, cooperate, deal with, empathize, get along with, help, interact, support, sympathize, work with.

SHARE (to share information): acknowledge, admit, air, announce, concede, confess, divulge, grant, impart, make known, mention, own up, report, reveal, say, state, tell.

SIMPLISTIC (in the sense of simple, even sometimes regrettably so): crude, elementary, fallacious, foolish, primitive, simple, simpleminded, simplified, spurious, superficial, thoughtless, uncomplicated.

Structure: arrange, array, build, classify, combine, compose, configure, construct, group, order, organize, put together, systematize.

Suggest: advance, advise, broach, hint, imply, offer, propose, put forward, recommend, submit.

Time-line: calendar, chronology, plan, program, schedule, sequence, tempo, timetable.

Top: best, champion, chief, choice, commanding, crowning, first, foremost, head, highest, important, leading, main, matchless, notable, outstanding, paramount, peerless, preeminent, premier, primary, prime, principal, ranking, second to none, superior, supreme.

Up to: as many as, at most, ending with, limited to, maximum of, no more than.

UTILIZE: Bring into play, employ, exploit, operate, resort to, set to work, try, use, wield.

VIABLE: feasible, possible, practicable, practical, robust, workable. As in a "viable" argument or explanation: defensible, reasonable, suitable, worthy of consideration.

PANOPLY: We have been reading and hearing *panoply* used in strange ways. On the television, a lawyer explaining legislation said, "Then the Congress has to go through every step—through the whole panoply of law-making."

RHD says that a *panoply* is either (1) a complete suit of armor or (2) a complete covering or array of something. AHD agrees, adding that the covering array should be "magnificent, shining." Webster III adds (3) a magnificent or impressive array (as *the full panoply of autumn foliage*) and (4) a display of all appropriate appurtenances. The core meaning seems to be trappings, habiliments, or coverings that impress the onlooker, the oldest meaning being restricted to armor. Not even Webster, however, suggests using *panoply* to mean a sequence, a passing show, or a parade.

PARALLELISM: Words, phrases, clauses, or sentences can come in a series in which each member gives an equal and parallel part of the meaning:

> The groups were of three kinds: male, female, and mixed.

The three items in the series are expressed in the same way—three adjectival forms, all having the same syntactical connection to the first part of the sentence. Here are some ways the parallelism could have been ruined:

> . . . male, a female, and mixed.
> . . . a male group, female, and a mixed.
> Males composed one of the three kinds of groups, which also included a female group and a mixed.

> After having experts go over the items in the first draft, revising the items, pretesting with 50 children in a local school, performing an item analysis, revising again, and printing final forms, we took the questionnaires to the schools of our sample for final use.

That last example has six phrases, each beginning with a participle: *having, revising, pretesting, performing, revising, and printing.* The parallelism could have been ruined in any number of ways; for example:

> After having experts go over the items in the first draft, we revised the items, then pretesting with . . .

> After experts went over the items in the first draft, the items were revised. Then after pretests in a local school, item analysis, revising again, and printing. . . .

Here is a sentence that goes wrong because of a lack of clear parallelism:

> At the present time, there is a dearth of specific information concerning the views and perceptions of school superintendents and others associated with public education relative to the extent and magnitude of the problems as well as positive interventions to alleviate the problems.

One difficulty is the antecedent of *as well as.* What is it? Another difficulty is that *concerning, relative to,* and *of* have similar functions in the sentence, and it is a puzzle to figure out how many of the words following them they are meant to affect. Taking out a few unnecessary words, changing a phrase to indicate better where it ends, and repeating a phrase for the sake of parallelism, we have:

> At present, there is a dearth of information about what superintendents and others associated with public education believe to be the extent and magnitude of the problem; there is also a dearth of intervention to alleviate the problems.

Readers always expect to find parallel ideas expressed in parallel form. Baker calls parallel construction "the masonry of syntax." Strunk and White (under "Express co-ordinate ideas in similar form") and the Ebbitts also give lucid advice. See also **ELEGANT VARIATION**.

PARAMETER, PERIMETER: *Parameter* is a mathematical term. RHD defines it as "a constant or variable term in a function that determines the specific form of the function but not its general nature, as a in $f(x) = ax$, where a determines only the slope of the line described by $f(x)$."

It is true that the parameter restricts the values that x can take, but *parameter* does not mean a limit or boundary in the ordinary sense. Too often, we encounter *parameter* used in the latter way, as "We have got to set parameters to the use of DDT" or "The bear paced the parameters of his cage." Probably both authors were thinking of *perimeter*. *Limits* would have served well in both sentences.

PHILOSOPHY has technical meanings and also common-language meanings. A technical meaning given by AHD is: "inquiry into the nature of things based on logical rather than empirical methods." One given by RHD is: "the critical study of the basic principles and concepts of a particular branch of knowledge, especially with a view to improving or reconstituting them."

AHD gives two meanings from more-general usage: "any system of motivating concepts or principles" and "a basic theory; a viewpoint: *an original philosophy of advertising.*" Sometimes, as in "All sixteen principals believed in the philosophy of student involvement," writers seem to use *philosophy* as synonymous with words such as *idea, logic, method, plan, program,* and *rationale,* in addition to AHD's *theory* and *viewpoint.*

Scholarly and technical writers, when writing about matters that approach the technical meanings of *philosophy,* might want to avoid using the word in its popular sense in the same article.

PLETHORA: After saying that there were a great many studies on a particular topic, an article in a psychological journal went on: "Sawyer reviewed a plethora of those studies." We think the author meant only that Sawyer reviewed a large portion of the studies; but what the sentence actually said, according to dictionaries, is that Sawyer reviewed more articles than he really cared to. A *plethora* is not merely a lot; it is an excess or superabundance.

PLURALS

1. Numbers and capital letters can form plurals without an apostrophe: "The Cs stand for corporations established during the 1960s. YMCAs are omitted." Similarly with proper names: "The Johnsons disagree. We must keep up with the Joneses." Lower-case letters and abbreviations containing periods need apostrophes: *x's, Ph.D.'s.* That is the advice of Fowler and the Chicago Manual.

2. Whether a singular or plural verb should be used with a collective noun depends on the sense. If you are talking about the collectivity as a unity, use the singular verb. If you are talking about the members as separate actors or things, use the plural: "The group from Hagerstown was the first to arrive" (compared as a unit to other groups). "The married

couple were glaring at each other." (*Was* would be absurd.)
"The number of chairs was too small" and "A number of
visitors were left standing."

3. Some plurals are unnecessary. Collective nouns do not
need to be made into plurals; indeed, many writers on usage
consider it gauche to do so. *Behavior* includes many acts.
Knowledge includes many things known. *Understanding* includes many insights. (This last has an exception in its use
in the sense of *agreements*: "During the negotiations, they
reached three separate understandings.") The plurals—be-
haviors, knowledges, understandings—irritate many readers.
The opposition to plurals of collective nouns, however, is not
unanimous. Although neither AHD nor RHD lists a plural
for *behavior*, Webster III does.

Just as the singular noun is customary in a phrase such
as *three kinds of apple*, so the singular noun is customary
when used as an adjective, as in *truck driver*. Yet nowadays
we encounter phrases like *skills training, values clarification*,
and *needs assessment*. That seems as unnecessary as to write
trucks driver, offices management, or *hats rack*.

PODIUM, LECTERN: Step up on the podium and put your
lecture notes on the lectern.

POSITIVE, NEGATIVE: Informally, and even in formal writing, *postive* has come into wide use as a synonym for *good*,
as in "I had a positive feeling." And *negative* has come to
mean *bad*. Let us review the options. Since *positive* and
negative are opposites, we will give chief attention to *positive*,
letting the uses of *negative* be implied.

The chief standard meanings of *positive* appearing in our
three dictionaries are these:

1. explicit, with little likelihood of misunderstanding: *a
positive specification of the requirements*. This is analogous to

the meaning in reference to machinery; that is, transmission of motion with no slippage between the moving parts: *a positive linkage;*

2. affirmation: a positive answer (yes);

3. admitting no doubt, irrefutable: *a positive proof;*

4. confident in opinion: *he is positive that he is right;*

5. increasing, making progress, going forward;

6. practical;

7. real;

8. absolute;

9. one pole or aspect of something, the other labeled negative; and

10. emphasizing what is laudable, hopeful, or to the good. A direction assumed to be beneficial, auspicious, or favorable: *a positive attitude, positive remarks about her performance, a positive trend in the mosquito population.* This meaning comes close to the current usage as *good.* It does not appear in AHD, but does appear in RHD and Webster III. RHD implies that this usage is less frequent than the others.

The dictionaries give other special meanings in the fields of biology, chemistry, electricity, grammar, machinery, mathematics, medicine, philosophy, and photography. We note, in passing, that the meaning in mathematics and statistics (one variable increasing when another increases) would give an opposite interpretation of the example about mosquito population in No. 10 above.

In sum, *positive* can be interpreted by readers in at least ten ways. The meanings of *negative* are correspondingly multiple. RHD uses five inches of column space for its entry on *positive* and four and one-half for *negative.* The multiplicity of meanings makes it easy to write sentences that leave the reader uncertain whether one meaning or another is meant. We give some examples culled from various places:

"A positive reaction was evident in all evaluations." Was that reaction undoubted, explicit (whether favorable or unfavorable), or was it one of affirmation?

"Although this trend can be viewed as positive . . ." The author meant that some people wanted the trend to continue; he was using the meaning of making progress, going forward. The reader familiar with other uses of *positive* could think he meant that the trend was increasing, that there was no doubt that it was occurring, or that the people engaged in it were confident about it.

"There are some positive developments." Were the developments unmistakable, increasing, or to the good?

"I am positively impressed with this book." Was the book reviewer happily impressed, or was he saying that he had no doubt about his impression, without saying whether it was favorable or unfavorable?

". . . when people do not perceive significant bases for positive relationships." What kind of relationships—explicit (whether good or bad), real, or laudable?

"This phenomenon is clearly distinguishable from the negative aspects of decision-making." Because of the wide use nowadays of *negative* as unfavorable, it is easy to interpret that sentence as referring to unhappy side-effects of a decision. Actually, the authors meant deciding *not* to act or deciding *not* to decide. Avoiding a decision, of course, can bring either happy or unhappy results.

"Professor Strunk was a positive man" is from White's introduction to Strunk and White. You can tell how he was using *positive* from his next sentence: "His book contained rules of grammar phrased as direct orders."

It may be that *positive* in the sense of *good* and *negative* in the sense of *bad* are becoming permanent usages. Or it may be that those usages are a fad. Vague synonyms for *good* and *bad* are typically faddish.

See also **GOOD** and **OVERUSED WORDS.**

POSITIVE AND NEGATIVE FEEDBACK: For a good many years, now, *feedback* has been a technical term in the application of principles of group dynamics to communication in natural groups. Susan is giving Howard *feedback* when she tells him the effect of his behavior or utterances on her. "Susan gave Howard positive feedback" means that Susan liked what Howard said or did.

Feedback comes from cybernetics and before that from radio circuitry. In a system with feedback channels, one or more features of the output are transmitted (fed back) to sensors connected to controls of the input. The feedback alters the input and consequently the output. In the language of cybernetics, if increases in the output cause the feedback to *decrease* the output, the feedback is called *negative* feedback. Negative feedback keeps the output of the system within bounds. If increases in the output cause the feedback to *increase* the input and then the output still further, the feedback is called *positive feedback.* Sometimes positive feedback increases levels of variables in the system to a range where negative feedback sets in and the system equilibrates in the new range. In other instances, runaway increase in the feedback loop continues until the system destroys itself.

In cybernetics, positive and negative have no evaluative connotations; neither is necessarily good or bad. But for the sake of making a contrast, let us assume that we do not like to see a system destroy itself. With that temporary assumption, we can say that in cybernetics, positive feedback is bad, negative good, But in the current jargon of applied group dynamics, the reverse holds: positive feedback is good, negative bad. The reason, presumably, is that *positive* has become so often used to mean *good* and because people usually like to be told that what they are doing is good. Without checking with the local cyberneticist, then, Howard can thank Susan for the positive (good, pleasing) feedback he got from her.

See also **OPEN SYSTEM; POSITIVE, NEGATIVE; SYSTEM.**

PRECISION

1. Even in technical writing, not every sentence need be precise. Introductory sentences often do their best work when they do not try to do too much. In bringing readers down to a fine point, you can do it in easy stages, letting each sentence narrow the focus a little more.

Having focused your readers' attention, you then come to the sentences in which you want to convey precise meanings. There, in addition to clear sentence structure, it is important to choose your words to have maximum likelihood of conveying the meaning you want.

First, choose words you think the greatest number of your readers are likely to understand—*popular* instead of *exoteric*, for example. Most writers on writing urge you to use simple, common words wherever you can. Doing so reduces the number of readers who will run away from your prose because they run away from big words, the number who will run with increasing annoyance to the dictionary, and the number who will finally throw down your article or book in resentment.

Second, when you come to one of your key words, ask yourself whether the meaning you intend is the only meaning your readers might put on the word. If you have any doubt at all, go to a dictionary, preferably two or three. If they do not satisfy you, go to two or three books on usage. Do not go to your friend across the street or your colleague down the hall. They are very likely to be wearing your same blinders of educational level or occupation. Go to the people who collect all the frequent uses of a word for your inspection: the makers of dictionaries and works on usage.

Be especially cautious about words that are especially popular, even overused, in your crowd or occupation. For example, see **IDENTIFY, POSITIVE, PRESENTING, SHARE,** and **OVERUSED WORDS.**

2. In the wish to be precise, writers in social science often overdo it. Here is an example; we have put in italics the words that could have been omitted.

> The cover letter, the critical incident packet, and the staff profile sheet will be mailed to *each of* approximately 300 extension staff members throughout the state. Respondents will be asked to *read and* rate each critical incident on effectiveness and to complete the staff profile sheets. *Upon completion of the aforementioned,* respondents will be asked to return the materials in a pre-addressed, pre-stamped envelope *to the researcher.* After two weeks, reminder cards will be sent *to respondents asking them to complete and return the packets.*

Did the researcher think the respondents might rate the items in the questionnaire without reading them? Did he worry that we might think he would ask respondents to return the questionnaires before filling them out? Did he think we might wonder to whom the pre-addressed envelopes were addressed or that we wouldn't be able to figure to what the reminder cards would remind the respondents to do? Apparently he did.

3. Finally, precision is not always the most important thing, despite the importance we give it in this book. Teachers of English composition sometimes cry, "If your writing is muddy, your thinking is muddy." Whether or not that is true, one unfortunately gets the impression that we should not write until our thinking is clear. But that is a terrible discouragement. Some thoughts are worth expressing before they are neat and orderly. Indeed, one of the best reasons for writing out our thoughts is to get help from others in sorting them out.

There is nothing wrong in being inexact or fuzzy if you do not pretend that you are being precise. Sometimes the best ideas emerge first in fuzzy forms. When the eminent physicist F. J. Dyson, then editor of *The Physical Review,* was asked how he could tell a crackpot manuscript from a break-through in physical theory, he wrote:

> The objection that they are not crazy enough applies to all the attempts which have so far been launched at a radically new theory of elementary particles. It applies especially to crackpots. Most of the crackpot papers which are submitted to *The Physical Review* are rejected, not because it is impossible to understand them, but because it is possible. Those which are impossible to understand are usually published. When the great innovation appears, it will almost certainly be in a muddled, incomplete, and confusing form. To the discoverer himself it will be only half-understood; to everybody else it will be a mystery. For any speculation which does not at first glance look crazy, there is no hope [Dyson, 1958, p. 80].

PRESENTING: We used to hear or read that someone would be a speaker at a convention, give a paper there, or speak there. Nowadays we hear or read that someone will be a *presenter* at a convention, *present* a paper there, or *present* there. The dictionaries tell us that *presenter* and *present* as a transitive verb (*present a paper*) are standard usage. They do not list *present* as an intransitive verb (*present at a convention*). Apparently the dictionary makers have not seen the word used that way. Perhaps they will see it before their next editions.

When we read of someone *presenting* at some gathering, the image from the ethologists' use of that term comes to mind. The *Encyclopedia of Psychology* gives its meaning this way:

> PRESENTING. . . . Showing the genital zone can have a soothing effect, be a greeting ceremony, or indicate a rank inside a hierarchy. Sexual presenting need not necessarily be intended for someone of the opposite sex. Male baboons of an inferior rank adopt female presenting behavior in front of a superior male. Strong males of the same species present their genitals when watching over the troop.

PRESUME: Sometimes authors use *presume* to mean *assume*, as in "This theory presumes that . . ." AHD says that the central meaning of *presume*, in its transitive sense, is "to take for granted, to assume to be true," but in its intransitive sense is "to act overconfidently, take liberties." AHD goes on to say that the central meaning of *presumption* is "behavior or language that is boldly arrogant or offensive." Some readers will interpret *presume* or *presumption* with the latter flavor. If you mean simply *assume*, then that word is safer.

PRETEST, POSTTEST: Spell them that way. No hyphens.

PREVALENT means occurring in many places, widespread. The emphasis is on space and conditions, not time. Not a synonym for *frequently*.

PROBLEMATIC has two uses. One is: having the character of a problem, posing a problem, difficult, as in "The routine work went smoothly; the problematic work ate up our time." The other is: doubtful, questionable, uncertain, as in "Even if the population surge arrives when predicted, and that is problematic, food supplies will be adequate."

It is easy to write sentences in which *problematic* is ambiguous; for example: "Resource allocation is problematic." That could mean either "Resource allocation is a problem" or "I doubt we will be able to allocate resources."

PUFFERY is the art of blowing things up larger than life. Technical and academic writers often make a thought sound larger, more important, more learned, more erudite, more recondite (see how our adjectives puff up as we go along?) than its actual content by their style of writing. Few writers, we are sure, practice puffery deliberately; it usually creeps in while the writer's attention is elsewhere.

1. A common form of puffery is the use of big words (we could have said *multisyllabic* words) when more common ones will do. (We could even have said that a common form of puffery is *sesquipedalianism*.) We are not disparaging the more formal words; we are not saying they are pretentious in themselves or that they ought forever to be foregone (we have just used three ourselves: *disparaging, pretentious,* and *foregone*). We only urge writers not to reject routinely the simpler words for the more formal. (On the other hand, see **VARIETIES OF USAGE** 3.) Here are some examples of formal words and phrases, followed by common ones that often convey the same meaning:

> acquire, obtain: get.
> at the present time, at this particular point in time: now.
> commence: begin, start
> define: describe. See **DEFINITIONS.**
> differentially: differently
> endeavor: try
> engage in dialog: talk
> identify: choose, pick, point out, name. See **IDENTIFY** and **OVERUSED WORDS.**
> implement: carry out. See **OVERUSED WORDS.**
> inception: beginning
> inculcate: teach
> initiate: begin
> in view of the fact that: because
> methodology: method. See **METHODOLOGY.**
> of great importance: important
> orientate: orient
> prior to: before
> simplistic: simple. See **SIMPLISTIC** and **OVERUSED WORDS.**
> utilize: use. See **OVERUSED WORDS.**
> viable: workable. See **VIABLE** and **OVERUSED WORDS.**
> visitation: visit. See **CONNOTATIONS.**

Flesch is death on big words. On page after page he says, "Don't use _____ when _____ will do." Here are a few of the heavier words he gives on his first few pages, with some of the more common words he offers to convey the same meanings:

accumulate: gather, collect
achieve: reach, do
additionally: besides, also, too
additional: more
adjacent: next
administer: give, run, manage
appropriate: proper
approximately: about
ascertain: find out

Now and then we encounter an article prefaced by an *executive summary.* We have yet to encounter a case where that seemed to mean anything more than *summary.*

2. Another form of puffery is to tell the reader over and over the importance of one's ideas. Some writers seem to have no plain, unadorned goals, but only *major* goals: *another major goal of the project was to* . . . They have no concepts except *key* concepts, no needs except *urgent* ones, and no ideas except *basic* ones. They make no distinctions that are not *pivotal* and no points that are not *vital, important,* or at least *worth noting.*

3. Fowler has a section on "genteelism," which he says is "the substitution of a synonym that is thought to be less soiled by the lips of the common herd." For example: *assist* for *help, desire* for *want, perspire* for *sweat.* See **EUPHEMISMS** and **THAT, WHICH.**

4. Some writers seem to feel, despite the standard rules of grammar, that *I* is more dignified than *me* and that adverbs are more refined than predicate adjectives. But ungrammatical expressions such as *between you and I* and *he felt badly* strip dignity from the author and dismay the reader.

5. Still another kind of puffery is sheer verbosity. This kind is so frequent that we give it a section of its own; see **WORDINESS.** But here is a choice example from Fowler

(under "abstractitis"): "A cessation of dredging has taken place" for "Dredging has stopped."

PUNCTUATION: See **APOSTROPHE, COLON, COMMA,** and **VIRGULE.**

QUALITY: Neither AHD nor Webster III lists *quality* as an adjective as in *quality cloth* and *quality education.* RHD does. Presumably AHD and Webster III are saying you will be more easily understood if you use a phrase such as *cloth of good quality* or *high-quality education.* It is, of course, always possible to use a noun as an adjective, but ambiguity sometimes arises; see **NOUNS AS ADJECTIVES.**

QUITE: Two of the uses of *quite* are almost contradictory. *Quite* is used to mean completely, thoroughly, or wholly, as in "She was not quite finished" or "He was quite the dandy." It is also used to mean considerably but *not* completely, as in "The room was quite warm." It is easy to write ambiguous sentences with *quite*: "He was quite satisfied" could mean either completely or not completely satisfied.

REAL has many meanings and is correspondingly difficult to use with precision. Unless the context is crystal clear, readers can easily think you had some other meaning in mind than the one you intended. "There is a real reason for participants sometimes to feel inadequate." Should we interpret that sentence to mean that the reason was factual, not imaginary? Or genuine, not counterfeit or pretended? Or indubitable, unquestionable? More ambiguity arises with phrases like *a real advance in* and *a real contribution to.* Those phrases can be interpreted in all the ways we mentioned in the previous example; in addition, authors sometimes seem to mean that the advance or contribution is large in degree or amount. That meaning does not appear in any dictionary.

Context can make it clear: "We wondered at the time whether their fatigue was feigned to cover anxiety, but several later events convinced us it was real."

REASON IS BECAUSE: *Because* means *for the reason that;* so if you use both *reason* and *because,* you are being redundant. Just drop out *the reason . . . is,* and your sentence will be all right:

> [The reason] they do it [is] because there is no one else to turn to.

Or you can drop *because:*

> The reason they do it is that there is no one else to turn to.

REASON WHY: Perhaps you find you have written: "We wanted to know the reason why the subjects acted as they did." *Reason why* is redundant. Instead of that, write *to know the reason the subjects acted* or *to know the reason that the subjects acted* or *to know why the subjects acted.*

RELATE: Some words carry little meaning in themselves and function mostly as a rallying point for other words in the sentence. *Connect, associate,* and *depend* are like that; we must find out from the rest of the sentence the nature of the connection and the things connected. Many of us have long treated *relate,* too, as one of those words. But we must now be careful not to run afoul of a widespread new usage.

The recent usage of *relate* is given by RHD as "to establish a social or sympathetic relationship with a person or thing." Webster III adds "to interact realistically: *to relate well to people." Webster's New Collegiate* adds the sense of responding favorably, as in "He can't relate to that kind of music." AHD labels the sense of interacting "in a meaningful or coherent fashion" as jargon, but AHD's *Second College Edition* gives that sense as standard.

We cannot be sure whether the new use of *relate* is a fad. We hope it is.

RELATION, RELATIONSHIP: All the dictionaries we have looked in give such overlapping definitions for *relation* and *relationship* that the two words seem indistinguishable. Sometimes, however, you may find yourself writing a piece of some length in which you have frequent occasion to refer to relations between variables and also to relationships between people or objects. In such a case, we offer the possibility of using the two terms as we have just used them: *relations* between variables and relation*ships* between people or objects, as in "In the groups where the interpersonal *relationships* had a long history, the *relation* between cohesiveness and productivity was stronger than in the recently established groups." That usage stretches no dictionary's definition, and it may add an increment of clarity when you must refer often to both kinds of association.

RELEASED TIME: The phrase means time released from regular duties. Perhaps because of the current predilection for using nouns as adjectives (see **NOUNS AS ADJECTIVES**), writers sometimes write *release time*. When you are about to type the phrase, remember that you are writing about time that is *released.*

REPRESENT: The map *represents* the territory. The sample *represents* the population. *Represent* belongs with the family of words containing *delineate, denote, depict, describe, exemplify, portray, signify, stand* or *act in place of.* It is wasted when used as a loose connective, as in "Start-up alone represents considerable time and energy." Start-up does not depict, exemplify, or act in place of time and energy. *Requires* would be better in that sentence. You stretch *represent* too much, also, when you use it merely as a polysyllabic synonym for *is*, as in "This represents a significant advance."

RÉSUMÉ: See **CURRICULUM VITAE.**

RHETORIC: The core meaning of *rhetoric* is simply the study or art of the effective use of language. Writers have long used the phrase "empty rhetoric" to mean exaggerated or inflated discourse, bombast. Presumably "empty" got lost, and many people now take *rhetoric* always to mean bombast.

ROLE is a technical term in sociology. When people have expectations about the way two persons should behave toward each other—about behavior that is required, permitted, and prohibited between them—and when the expectations are backed up by sanctions, then each of the persons is said to be in a role, or taking a role. Examples are the complementary roles between physician and patient, teacher and student, and so on. Obvious examples of role are those of job and occupation: physician, teacher, carpenter, business executive, and the like. But not all roles are jobs. Patient, student, husband, customer, lover, pedestrian, member of the audience in a theater are roles but not jobs. When you are writing about jobs, occupations, or positions in an organization, not about the much larger class of relationship denoted by *role*, you can be more precise by using *job, occupation,* or *position.*

RUBRIC means heading, not kind. *Under the rubric of* is a fancy way of saying *under the heading of.*

SCALE: See **CONTINUUM.**

SCENARIO once meant a synopsis. Nowadays, its meaning is closer to that of a script. Applied to planning or speculating about the future, it means a narrative in some detail telling one of the ways the consequences of acts taken now might play themselves out in the future. The word is often used for purposes of puffery (see **PUFFERY**). If you mean merely a plan, prediction, possibility, or alternative, use one of those words, not *scenario.*

SEX: See **GENDER.**

SEXIST LANGUAGE

1. Awkwardness with pronouns can usually be avoided by using the plural or by repeating the original noun. You can write: "If researchers want to be sure of welcome in schools, they should start making arrangements some months in advance" instead of "If a researcher . . . , he or she should . . ." You can write: "The researcher who wants maximum control over relevant variables must accept in exchange a lowered generalizability to natural settings; the researcher cannot have both." If you are willing to write in the second person (as we are doing here), you can write: "If you want maximum control . . ." If none of those techniques will work, fall back on *he or she.*

2. Instead of *man* (as in *man has had a long history of* . . .) and *mankind,* use *humans, humankind,* or *people.* See **HUMAN.**

3. You may not like giving up the long custom of using the masculine forms to stand for both men and women. If you go on using them, however, you should expect some of your readers to resent your doing so. For more detail on nonsexist language, see the Ebbitts and the Morrises.

4. Giving up the use of *he* to stand for both sexes, some authors have at the same time given up the agreement in

number between subject and verb—writing, for example, *If a researcher wants to be welcome, they should start . . .* We have found no need to do that in this book or in any other.

SHALL, WILL

I *will*, we *will*, you *will*, he, she, it *will*, they *will*. That is today's general usage, from children writing themes to professors writing for scholarly journals. The Morrises quote James Thurber's remark of some years ago: "Men who use *shall* west of the Appalachians are the kind who twirl canes and eat ladyfingers."

In the older usage, simple futurity was expressed by I or we *shall* and by you, he, she, it, or they *will*. Exchanging the *shall* for *will* or vice versa expressed determination, obligation, or command: "You shall appear promptly at eight o'clock." That usage is moribund, though not dead. The distinction between *shall* and *will* still appears, AHD says, in expressly formal usage, though it is "not closely observed in general usage, including much serious writing." RHD says the distinction appears "in formal speech and writing, as well as in the informal speech of some educated speakers." RHD also says that *shall* has fallen into disuse in ordinary speech. It still remains, however, in a few idiomatic expressions such as "Shall I go first?"

Legal language is always a century or so out of date, and it customarily uses *shall* to express obligation in the third person: "The party of the first part shall pay to the party of the second part . . ."

Don't use *shall* merely in the hope that it will give a formal or highly educated tone to your writing. The result is often ludicrous. Some time back we received a printed form asking for information about a friend who was applying for a job. The form said, "The applicant shall appreciate your completing this form." That meant that the person who sent the form was going to make sure that our friend appreciated what we wrote on the form. We recently found this sentence in a book: "The nature of socialism shall be discussed in Chapter 11." The author seemed to be commanding himself not to forget to discuss socialism in Chapter 11. See also **VARIETIES OF USAGE.**

SHARE: When you share a cookie, you must break it into shares, one for each person. When you share an automobile, you must use it jointly with others; it is no good to any if you break it into parts. Those are the two core meanings of *share.* AHD puts it this way: (a) to divide and parcel out in shares, (b) to participate in, use, or experience in common. No dictionary says that *share* in synonymous with *impart* or *tell.*

A friend came into our office recently with a letter in his hand, saying, "I want to share this letter with you." Curmudgeons that we are, we asked whether our share was to be the top or the bottom half of the letter.

In a television broadcast on 7 June 1981, Ronald Reagan said, "I wanted to share this decision with you as soon as possible." He did not mean that he was eager for the rest of us to help him make the decision. He meant merely that he wanted to tell us the decision he had already made.

We hope the fad for using *share* to mean *impart, reveal,* or *tell* will be short-lived. See also **OVERUSED WORDS.**

SIMPLISTIC refers to a tendency to oversimply, to ignore inherent complexities. A *simplistic* treatment of a topic damages understanding by omitting complexities necessary to understanding. A *simple* treatment quickens understanding by omitting unnecessary subtopics, using common language wherever possible, and hewing to the essentials. Using *simplistic* as a fancy synonym for *simple* weakens *simplistic.* See **OVERUSED WORDS** and **PUFFERY.**

SLANT (/) or **SOLIDUS:** See **VIRGULE.**

SPEAK TO: A locution frequent in academic writing is *speak to*, as in *Johnson speaks to the problem of whether* . . . and *The findings of Johnson and Johnson also speak to the question of* . . .

Speak to is a rarefied pedantry. It is easy to avoid if you care to do so. In the first example above, substitute *about* for *to* or *writes about* for *speaks to*. In the second example, substitute *clarify, cast light on, illuminate, simplify, are relevant to,* or some such phrase for *speak to*. Here is an example from a book review and its revision:

> This volume speaks importantly to a number of issues central to all science and does this well. [Instead use: This volume says important things about a number of issues central to all science and says them well.]

See also **IMPORTANT** and **PUFFERY.**

STRESS has four core meanings: (1) the accent given a syllable or a word, (2) emphasis, or directing special attention to an idea or perception, (3) a force that tends to strain or deform, and (4) a disruption of physical, mental, or emotional equilibrium in an animal, including the human; distress.

1. Writers sometimes use *stress* in a way that leaves the reader wondering whether the author means an emphasis or a straining force. For example:

> We must conclude that the theory places great stress on the formal curriculum and on the program of instruction.

Does that mean that using the theory would threaten the integrity of ordinary conceptions of curriculum and instruction? No, the author means merely that curriculum and instruction figure prominently in the theory. You can often avoid ambiguity by using *accent, accentuate, emphasize, feature, highlight, point up,* or *underscore.*

2. To make it clear whether you mean, on the one hand, that a person or thing is under pressure or, on the other hand, that it is actually bent out of shape, you can borrow a distinction from engineering. To mechanical engineers, *stress* means the deforming force, and *strain* means the amount of deformation in the object being stressed.

SUCH must refer to something already stated or about to be stated or implied. When used to refer backward, *such* means *of that kind,* and the kind must have been stated or implied. Here are some examples in which *such* added nothing but four letters to the authors' sentences:

> Some theorists also recognize the potential of people to adapt to their circumstances, though such adaptation is . . .

Since no particular kind of adaptation was mentioned, *such* is superfluous. Better would have been: *though their adaptation is . . .*

> We were then ready for the next stage. It seemed best to begin such a stage . . .

Such as what? Such as a next one? Better would have been: *it seemed best to begin it . . .*

> Decision making requires adequate information, and too often those in authority lack such information.

Better would have been: *and too often those in authority lack it.*

> A given culture may add external rewards and pressures to tasks to compensate for the culturally devalued properties of such tasks. Such practices may lead to a generalized negative association between paying for the task and its inherent enjoyment.

Presumably that means "When tasks are looked down upon, a culture may make them more attractive with special rewards and pressures." People then come to believe that "a paid-for task is unlikely to be enjoyable."

SURVIVE: *Outlive, outlast,* and *survive* all mean to exist longer than some other person or thing. *Survive* has the flavor of continued existence in the face of threat or after a dangerous experience: "He survived the wreck." "She survived the tyrannies of her teachers." "The ordeal taxed his every sinew, but he survived it."

Since *survive* means for one person or thing to outlast another, your sentence will be clearer if you state the person or thing that the other person or thing is outlasting, as in the examples above. Avoid *survive* without an object, as in: "If you want to survive, you must work hard." Survive what or whom? The sentence is grammatical, but vague.

SYSTEM: Dictionaries distinguish four general meanings of *system*. Three of them correspond to technical usage in social science. Since the term has several rather distinct meanings, some or all of which will be familiar to your readers, it is important to give readers some clue to the meaning you intend.

1. Probably the simplest meaning, most frequent in general usage, is any orderly arrangement or procedure, anything systematic, as in "They have a system for checking on things."

2. Another meaning is that of a conceptual system, an assemblage of related ideas, as *a system of philosophy*. This usage is common among theoreticians in social science, although not among physical scientists.

3. The third meaning is different from the first chiefly in its emphasis on complex human action: a coordinated body of methods or a complex scheme for carrying out a task.

This usage is applied frequently to life in complex modern organizations: *systems analyst, systems technology, control systems, information systems, management systems, office systems, a system for paper flow.*

4. In a nutshell, the fourth meaning specifies that the whole is greater than the sum of its parts. Dictionaries put it something like this: an assemblage of interacting parts forming a unitary whole, as in a *railroad system, a school system.* We can be more precise by paraphrasing Miller (1978, p. 16): a set of interacting units with relationships among them, the units having some common properties and each depending for its function on at least some others, and the whole having at least one measure that is larger than the sum of the measures of its units.

Since the fourth meaning has become widespread in the literature of social science, especially in social psychology, sociology, human ecology, economics, and the like, it is important to write so that context makes your usage clear. Without further explanation, a sentence such as "They built a system to carry out that function" can leave the reader wondering whether you intend the first, third, or fourth meaning of *system.*

In recent years, a fifth meaning of *system* has come into wide use; it appears most often in the terms *general systems* and *general system(s) theory.* Probably the two best-known proponents of general system theory are Ludwig von Bertalanffy and James G. Miller. "General systems theory," writes Miller (1978, p. 9), "is a set of related definitions, assumptions, and propositions which deal with reality as an integrated hierarchy of organizations of matter and energy. General living systems theory is concerned with a special subset of all systems, the living ones." Miller distinguishes seven levels of living systems: cell, organ, organism, group, organization, society, and supranational system. General system theory seeks behavior that can be described in the same way at different levels of system, and it seeks hypotheses that can be tested at more than one level. See also **OPEN SYSTEM.**

TABLE, FIGURE, CHART, EXHIBIT label different kinds of displays.

1. Minimally, a *table* is a list. Usually, it is a rectangular array. It usually contains numbers, but not always. This is a table:

Table 1

	Before	After
Level 1	1.39	2.67
Level 2	0.76	1.22
Level 3	−3.72	−0.34

So is this:

Table 2

	Level 1	Level 2	Level 3
Group 1	female	mixed	male
Group 2	female	female	mixed

2. The label *figure* can be used for anything other than a table. It is usually a picture, diagram, or graph. See **DIAGRAM** for one type of figure. Figure 2 is another.

Figure 2

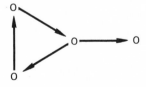

3. A *chart* is usually a map. The label can also be used for a diagram, as for an organization chart.

4. The label *exhibit* can substitute for any of the other three terms. Exhibits are usually put on separate sheets, and

they are usually collected at the end of a document, like appendices.

5. A table or other display that reads the usual way on a page is called *vertical*. If it is too wide and must be turned to read the long way on the page, it is called a *side turn* or *broadside*. It is customary among printers to turn a broadside table so that you push the book to the left and turn your head to the left to read it.

TAKE, BRING: See **BRING, TAKE.**

TANDEM means in train, one after the other, end to end, not beside or at the same time.

TEND: If you *tend* to do something, you are disposed, inclined, or likely to do it. If you *tend* toward something, you bear toward it or head toward it. "He tended to get angry at that kind of question." "The women in the group tended to support one another."

Authors sometimes use *tend* to indicate an average or a majority, giving the word a meaning something like *on the average it was the case that* or *in most instances it was the case that*. When *tend* is applied to a collectivity in that manner, strange meanings can result. Here is an instance: "Members of the group tended to be male." That sentence sent our imaginations reeling as we pictured members of that group inclining toward being male.

Here are two more instances of ambiguity. "The older subjects tended to have more favorable opinions." Was every one of the older subjects favorably disposed, did a majority of them have favorable opinions, or on the average did the older subjects have opinions that were more favorable than those of the younger subjects? Finally: "Most citizens have tended not to possess high degrees of knowledge." Does that mean that among most citizens, each of them has been disposed to avoid acquiring a high degree of knowledge, or that a majority of citizens have not possessed a high degree of knowledge?

You can avoid ambiguity by using *tend* to refer only to the inclinations of individuals or to inclinations in collectivities that require joint action to be visible. See the examples in our first paragraph.

TERMS: See **IN TERMS OF.**

THAN I OR ME? When you wonder whether to use the nominative or the objective case after *than,* simply fill in the missing words. "You know him better than I" means that you know him better *than I do.* "You know him better than me" means that you know him better *than you know me.*

THAT, THIS: See **THIS, THAT.**

THAT, WHICH: "To this day," Bernstein says, "there are those who seem to feel that *which* is more stately." Stately or not, using *that* in some places and *which* in others can clarify the meaning you want a clause to give to the rest of the sentence.

A clause is a complete sentence that is tacked onto another sentence and fastened to it by some sort of connecting word or punctuation mark, or both. The simplest example is a clause fastened to the main sentence by a conjunction; for example: "_____ , but the time wasn't ripe." The clause *the time wasn't ripe* is a complete sentence in itself. It is fastened to the main sentence by the conjunction *but.* See **COMMA 6.**

Another way to connect a clause to the main sentence is to use a pronoun as the subject of the clause, letting the pronoun refer to a noun that appears in the main sentence. *That* and *which* often serve as pronouns for that purpose. For example: "We wanted to use the large room, which was at the end of the hall." *Which* is the subject of the clause. It refers to *room* in the main sentence. Clauses can also be put in the middle of a sentence: "The large room, which was at the end of the hall, suited our needs."

Clauses attached with commas give one meaning to the main sentence; clauses attached without commas give another. For example: "We wanted to use the large room, which was at the end of the hall." The essential meaning in that sentence is contained in the main part of it: "We wanted to use the large room." The added clause gives more information, but it could be put in parentheses or dropped entirely without hurting the sense of the first part of the sentence. That kind of clause is called a *nonrestrictive* clause, because it does not narrow the meaning of what it refers to. If the clause were dropped, the reader would still know what room we wanted to use.

Not so in this example: "We wanted to use the large room that was at the end of the hall." That sentence tells us that there was more than one large room, and the one we wanted was the one at the end of the hall. The clause in that sentence is called a *restrictive* clause; without it, the reader would not know which large room we wanted to use.

Note that we used the pronoun *which* as the subject of the nonrestrictive clause and put a comma before it. We used the pronoun *that* as the subject of the restrictive clause and did not put a comma before it. APA, Baker, Bernstein, the Chicago Manual, Copperud, the Ebbitts, Fowler, the Morrises, Strunk and White, the Council of Biology Editors (1978), and the American Medical Association (Barclay, Southgate, and Mayo, 1981) all advise this use of *that*, *which*, and the comma.

One more example to be sure we are clear. "The room, which was at the end of the hall, suited our needs." The clause is enclosed in commas, and it begins with *which; that means the room suited our needs*, and (by the way) it was at the end of the hall. But now: "The room that was at the end of the hall suited our needs." The clause is *not* separated from the rest of the sentence by commas, and it begins with *that*. The clause tells which room suited our needs; namely, the one at the end of the hall.

This simple rule will clarify a great many sentences: use *that* without a comma when the clause is necessary to the meaning of the main sentence; use *which* with a comma when you can put the clause in parentheses or drop it without seriously bending the main sentence.

We are omitting some subtleties about using *that* and *which*, but they can be found in any of the books on usage we have cited. We have given space here to the distinction we think most often makes trouble for writers. See also **COMMA** 6.

THEORY: Many social scientists hesitate to claim they are writing *theory*. We see titles of articles, even books, like *An Approach to a Theory of . . ., Notes Toward a Theory of . . .,* and *A Prolegomenon to a Theory of . . .* Instead of *theory*, we see words and phrases that mean about the same thing: *Conceptual Framework for, Some Principles of, Model of.* Rarely do we see a title that says straight out: *A Theory of . . .*

Perhaps some social scientists yearn for a Theory That Sweeps Away All Others. Perhaps they avoid being accused of overweening ambition by claiming not to be writing a Theory, but only a conceptual framework or a model. We think it too bad to reserve *theory* to mean only Good Theory or Grand Theory or Unassailable Theory. We would like writers to feel free to use *theory* whenever they are theorizing. Modesty is all very well, but leaning over too far backward removes a good word from currency.

Theory belongs to the family of words that includes *guess, speculation, supposition, conjecture, proposition, hypothesis, con-*

ception, explanation, model. The dictionaries permit us to use *theory* for anything from "guess" to "a system of assumptions, accepted principles, and rules of procedure devised to analyze, predict, or otherwise explain the nature or behavior of a specified set of phenomena" (AHD). Social scientists will naturally want to use terms with more care than they are used by the general populace. They will naturally want to underpin their *theories* with more empirical data than they need for a *speculation.* They will naturally want a *theory* to incorporate more than one *hypothesis.* We plead only that they do not save *theory* to label their ultimate triumph, but use it as well to label their interim struggles.

About 25 years ago, the *Psychological Review* published a spoof, a satire, entitled *Side-Steps Toward a Non-Special Theory.* Under "Personality," it explained the pervasive effects of umbilical trauma. Under "Mathematical Psychology," it described the universal applicability of the arithmetic mean, and so on. The article brought the *Review* more letters than usual, but few writers-in were pleased. Most complained about frivolity, even sacrilege. To the best of our knowledge, the *Review* has not published another spoof.

Physical scientists display a sense of humor about their theorizing. They give fanciful names to atomic particles like *charm* and *quark.* One phenomenon is named after the Red Queen in *Alice Through the Looking-Glass.* If social scientists are not yet ready to borrow names from Lewis Carroll, we hope they can at least relax their scrupulosity about *theory.*

See also **ATTEMPT** and **MODEL** and **PUFFERY.**

THINK: See **BELIEVE, FEEL, THINK.**

THIS IS BECAUSE: Two troubles arise with *this is because.* One is the likely ambiguity about the antecedent of *this* when the pronoun is meant to refer to the action in a previous sentence, not merely to a noun near its end (see **THIS, THAT**). The other is the misleading *is*. Almost never does the author who writes *this is because* mean to give a reason for something being or existing (*is*). Almost always, the author wants to say that what happened in the previous sentence did so because so-and-so, or what was asserted in the previous sentence is true because so-and-so, or the like. Instead of "This is because the experimental design is inadequate," one can write:

> This is so because . . .
> That is the case because . . .
> That happens because . . .
> The reason is that . . .
> The reason is the inadequacy of the experimental design.

Here is an actual example:

> Path models rarely include experimental variables, even though they could be exogenous variables in a model. This is because of the problems that polytomies present in analysis.

And a recasting:

> Because of the problems that polytomies pose in analysis, path models rarely include . . .

THIS, THAT: Here are some excerpts from a page and a half of an article about sociology written by a sociologist (the italics are ours, for a reason we'll explain later):

> the present market situation has forced *our* profession to make some concessions. . . . However, *it* has not always been the case. . . . However, *the* early reformism too often took on a patronizing, "do-gooder" attitude. . . . In the subsequent drive to establish sociology . . . *the* interest in melioristic interventions gave way to a more objective instrumentalism. . . . Wirth detailed the nature and manner of *the* early clinical sociology. . . . few sociologists today are even aware of *that* chapter in our history. Nevertheless, a few individuals struggled to maintain *the* clinical tradition. . . . The eclipse of *the* tradition seems, at last, to be at an end.

. . . most of *the* new crop of sociological clinicians emerged in isolation from one another.

Now go back through those quoted excerpts, and substitute *this* wherever you find an italicized word; every one of them was *this* in the original. That will give you a feeling for the excessive use of *this* into which many writers have fallen.

Sometimes *this* peppering a page merely raises one's hackles. But sometimes it confuses:

> The *pièce de résistance* is the massive and scholarly *Sociobiology* by E. O. Wilson. This writer found . . .

Who is "this writer"—Wilson or the author of the sentence? Since that author, like the author of our first example, made no distinction between *this* and *that*, we had no clue until we read on and deduced the identity of "this writer" from later phrases.

Sometimes writers use the pronoun *this* (or *that*) to refer not to a noun used previously, but to the gist of a previous sentence. For example: "We begin with a brief statement of O'Keefe's theory of cultural reproduction. This will enable us . . ." For what does *this* stand? The authors did not mean that O'Keefe's theory of cultural reproduction would enable us to do something. They meant that beginning with a brief statement of it would enable us to do something. Better than *this* would have been *Doing so will enable us* . . . or *Restating the theory will enable us* . . .

When we talk or write about things in space, usage remains what it has been in living memory, and it remains the same in all varieties of usage: *this* and *that* are parallel in direction to *near* and *far*, *here* and *there*, *bring* and *take*, *come* and *go*, even *now* and *then*. *This* thing is close by, perhaps within reaching distance, in front of us, within view. *That* thing is far away, beyond reach, behind us, out of sight. Extending that usage to hearing, *this* sound or voice is what we are hearing now "What's this I hear?" or what we expect to hear

immediately. *That* is what we heard—"What's that again?"—
or may hear sometime in the future. In the dimension of
time, *this* time is now or the moments sweeping in to become
the present: "These are the times that try men's souls"; it is,
so to speak, the time close by, in front of us, within immediate
anticipation. *That* time is behind us or well on ahead: "That
was a time of dread." "That will be time enough."

Those metaphors of near and far, and so on, are useful in
the flow of writing. You can help your reader when you refer
backward and forward if you use *that* to refer to what you
have finished saying and *this* to what you are now saying or
are just about to say. That is the point of this section.

We wrote *That is the point* in the previous sentence, because
we were referring *back* to ideas already set down. We wrote
this section, because we were referring to the section in which
our readers now find themselves. If we were to refer to a
later section, we would write *that section*, because it would
be at a distance, not at our fingertips.

We saved a particularly annoying example for the final
one: *in the context of these foregoing statements*. Since the
statements were foregoing, they were behind the reader and
completed, not still being made, and the clearer word would
have been *those*. But in this case *those* would have been
redundant; *those* points behind us, and so does *foregoing*. The
best word in that sentence would have been neither *these*
nor *those*, but *the*. See also the substitutions in our first
example.

You may want to use *this* as frequently as the sociologist
we quoted so as to sound like your colleagues (see **AUDI-
ENCES**), or you may not. If you want to write with more
precision and variety, look back over your pages. Wherever
you see *this* or *these*, check whether it would be clearer,
simpler, smoother, or less pedantic to write *that, those, the,
I, we, he, she, it, they, them, here,* or *there*. Check *that* and
those, too, for possible substitution of *the, I, we,* etc.

THUSLY: AHD says that *thusly* "is occasionally employed humorously, for mock-stylish effects." Ninety-seven percent of its usage panel find *thusly* unacceptable. (See **USAGE PANELS.**) The Morrises say that " 'thus' is stuffy enough for all normal purposes." See also **FIRSTLY, FIRST OF ALL;** see also **IMPORTANT.**

TRANSPIRE: At one time, *transpire* was a technical term known only to botanists. Then it became accepted by writers on usage in the sense of *become known.* Now it is used widely in both general and formal writing as a synonym for *happen, occur, take place.* Those words seem good and sufficient to us, and we are sorry that *transpire* has been added to them, losing its former meaning. But unfortunately, if you write "It transpired that the experimenters were married," most readers will think you mean "It happened that the experimenters were married," not "It became known that the experimenters were married."

UNDER WAY: Two words, and don't spell it *under weigh.*

UNIQUE: Some words denote a condition that either exists or doesn't exist. They don't make good sense when you put *more* and *less* in front of them. Some examples are *absolute, final, unanimous,* and *unique.* If a thing is *unique,* it is the only one of its kind. It can't be *very* so or *more* so.

A purveyor of hi-fi discs advertised one as *a recording of music by two very different composers who shared a unique ability.* But if both of them had it, the ability wasn't unique to either one of them.

USAGE PANELS: AHD and the Morrises both selected panels of writers to help them comment on usage. We have cited in this book the votes of those panels on certain usages. One might question whether the writers on the panels actually write with the usages they told AHD or the Morrises they preferred to use. Maybe they felt the spotlight was on them, and maybe they sometimes yielded to the temptation to state a preference they felt was more "correct" than their own actual usage. We can't know the extent to which that happened; and in any case, it may be irrelevant. Regardless of how close their statements were to their own practice, maybe the members of the panels were telling us how they would like *us* to write. That seems to us a good enough reason to cite their preferences here.

Table 3 shows the compositions of the two panels. We classified the members as best we could from the brief descriptions given. Where we could have put a person in more than one category, we guessed at the category in which the person had spent the most time.

Table 3

	Number of persons	
	AHD	Morrises
Writers for general audiences (novels, non-fiction trade books, magazines, newspapers)	17	41
Writers of plays, poetry, history, and other humanities, and critics	18	25
Editors	22	22
Columnists	9	12
Correspondents, journalists	1	15
Professors of English	9	2
Professors of journalism	3	0
Other professor, curators	14	4
College presidents	1	3
Politicians	5	0
Lawyers	1	3
Clergy	1	2
Advertising writer	1	0
Judge	0	1
Librarian	1	0
Other	3	3
	106	133

Zinsser was one of the panelists for AHD. He says the guardians of usage have two jobs. One is to keep the language from becoming sloppy; the other is "to help the language grow by welcoming any immigrant that will bring strength or color" (p. 38).

On the one hand, Zinsser was happy that 95 percent of the panel voted against *myself* as in "He invited Mary and myself to dinner," that the panel voted heavily against using *cohort* to mean *colleague* and against *too* to mean *very*, and that the panel "strictly upheld most of the classic distinctions in grammar" such as between *can* and *may* and between *fewer* and *less*.

On the other hand, Zinsser was proud that 97 percent of the panel voted to accept *dropout* ("which is clean and vivid") into standard usage, and that large majorities of the panel accepted once-colloquial verbs like *stall, trigger,* and *rile,* the adjective *rambunctious,* and new words such as *moonscape, printout, pantyhose, wetlands, biodegradable,* and *uptight.*

Zinsser ends his chapter on usage with this:

> Prayerfully this chapter will help you to approach the question of "What is good usage?" but fearfully you will sometimes slide off the track. And if that sentence doesn't explain why "hopefully" is bad usage, go back to "Go." Do not collect $200.

See also **AUDIENCES, CHANGES IN USAGE** 1 and 3, **HOPEFULLY,** and **VARIETIES OF USAGE** 1.

UTILIZE: Follett says:

> Yet some words at some times and others at all times can be shown to be unnecessary. *Utilize* is one of the second class. . . . if *utilize* and *utilization* were to disappear tomorrow, no able writer of the language would be the poorer.

Write *use* instead. See also **OVERUSED WORDS.**

VARIABLES, DEPENDENT AND INDEPENDENT: See **DE-PENDENT AND INDEPENDENT VARIABLES.**

VARIETIES OF USAGE: Dictionaries and books on usage distinguish varieties of usage with labels like standard, non-standard, general, formal, informal, colloquial, slang, archaic, and obsolete. They use still other labels for the special vocabularies of various occupations and sciences. American dictionaries note special usages in regions of the U.S.A. and in other English-speaking countries. The compilers and authors do not presume to declare one usage correct and another incorrect. They provide the labels to tell us that readers of a certain kind of writing will have their ears set for that certain kind of usage. Readers of a novel will expect to find the characters speaking with informal, colloquial, and slang terms. Readers of a theoretical discourse in standard English, however, will have their attention snagged by a term of one of those sorts and will react with annoyance or delight depending on the skill of the writer.

1. Dictionaries and books on usage are, of course, the best guides to varieties of usage—not Shakespeare, Thomas Jefferson, Hemingway, teachers, friends, or even the writers in the journal in which one may aspire to publish. It would be best if we could test writing styles against a sample of our eventual readers. Without systematic access to that sample, however, the next best thing is to consult dictionaries and usage books. Although the compilers and authors of those books do not take random samples of readerships, at least they make a deliberate effort to remain aware of ranges of usage by constantly collecting samples of it. When a new dictionary is compiled, hundreds and even thousands of usage samples back up the meaning given for almost every word.

No individual or book can be the final authority on the usages that belong together in a particular variety of English.

That becomes clear when we look at several dictionaries and usage books. For example, *contact* is sometimes used as a verb to mean to get in touch with or communicate with. Baker tells us flatly, and so do Strunk and White, not to *contact* anyone, but to call, write, find, tell, phone, meet, get in touch with, or look up the person. AHD says the use of *contact* as a verb is informal; 66 percent of AHD's usage panel find the usage unacceptable in formal writing. Similarly, 65 percent of the Morrises' panel reject the usage in writing (see **USAGE PANELS**). Bernstein says the word can be useful when you don't want to be specific about the medium of communication, although a "practiced writer" can do very well without it. The Ebbitts say that *contact* as a verb is gaining acceptance in nonbusiness contexts, but that it remains rare in formal usage. Copperud says the word is coming into wider use as a verb (and Bernstein and RHD agree with that), although it "has not yet fully emerged into the sunshine of full acceptance, and is still partly in the shadow of its commercial origin." RHD says that many teachers and editors object to the usage, but it lists *contact* as a verb without any label restricting its use. Webster III simply lists the word as standard in the meaning of *reach*. In summary, the authorities range all the way from *don't use it* to *use it.*

We don't advise counting the number of writers for and against. Makers of dictionaries have already counted their thousands of noses, but even they must make some interpretation of shades of meaning and frequencies. Writers of books on usage work from dictionaries and their own experiences; but they go on to add their own opinions about what will make writing clear. However their collections of examples may tally, lexicographers must inevitably interpret their examples through their own understanding of words. Similarly, when you go to the lexicographers for guidance, you must balance what they say against your own style and your own audience. You can't simply take a vote.

What it comes down to is that no authority can give you a license to use a word without thinking about your audience, and no authority can take a word away from you if, after thinking over the use you want to make of it, you think it will be effective. Your decision will depend on your judgment of the usage current in your audience and on whether you want to stay with that usage or step out in front of it. Your decision will also depend on whether you are seeking a special effect (see below).

2. The clearest writers draw sharp attention in one way or another to their key ideas and let attention linger less upon the subordinate ideas. They do that through their organization of the piece as a whole and through their paragraph structure, but they do it also within sentences. One way to point up a key idea is to shift into a different variety of usage. We give here, first, an example of a sentence that sticks to formal usage and then, second, a rewriting of it in words in general usage except for one technical term.

The first sentence comes from an article in which the author was arguing that certain ways of running an organization draw out infantile behavior from the members. The author first explained what he meant by infantile versus adult behavior, and then what he meant by a "formal" organization. Then he wrote:

> From the organizational model above, it was possible to hypothesize that the more the organization approximates the properties of a formal organization, the more individuals will be required to seek expression of needs that approximates the infant end of the continua.

Our rewriting:

> If organizations work in the way I have described, then it follows that formal organizations will press people into behaving like children.

In that sentence, the one technical term is *formal organizations.* The sentence makes it clear that formality in organizations is connected to childish behavior and, because *formal organizations* is the only technical term, the sentence also makes it clear that we are using the term because it will be important later on.

Here is another example. The introductory section of an article written in formal language for the *Administrative Science Quarterly* ended with this paragraph:

> This article discusses what kinds of process exist, how processes interact with one another, and how organizational designs can be constructed from interacting processes. First, it is necessary to assess the designers' role and the objectives designers pursue.

Following that paragraph came this heading for the next section: WHY DESIGNERS SHOULD HELP OTHER PEOPLE ERECT AN ORGANIZATIONAL TENT. That heading captures one's fancy. One is eager to read on. Although the effect comes partly from the implied question in the heading and partly from its informal syntax, the chief part of the effect comes from the sudden appearance of *tent.* The word surprises us. Its meaning surprises us; we do not expect to come upon *tents* in a rather abstract article about organizations (the article has no special reference to circuses or carnivals). Its usage surprises us; we come upon that concrete word of general usage after several paragraphs of formal and technical prose. The effect makes us feel that something unusual and engaging is about to happen.

3. Feel free to use a word now and then that your readers may not know. If all writers were to use only words they are sure almost all of their readers will know, the language would soon shrink to the basic 600 words.

If you need a rare word, or even if you want to use it merely because you like the sound of it, and if you are going to use it only once or twice, you can usually arrange for the context to show a sufficient flavor of its meaning. For example, *embrangle* has nice onomatopoetic ring, and the sentences below give a good enough clue to its meaning:

> Automobiles sometimes baffle the efforts of even the best mechanics. Bees sometimes sting experienced keepers. Cats often foil efforts to train them. Even a lone, inexperienced child can embrangle the influence attempts of adults.

See also **AUDIENCES** and **CHANGES IN USAGE** and **USAGE PANELS.**

VERBAL: See **ORAL, VERBAL.**

VIABLE comes from the Latin *vita,* meaning life. It is cognate with *vital* and *vitality.* AHD gives it these chief meanings: (1) Capable of living, as a newborn infant or fetus reaching a state of development that will permit it to survive and develop under normal conditions. (2) Capable of living, developing, or germinating under favorable conditions, as seeds, spores, or eggs. (3) Capable of actualization, as a project; practicable. Webster III goes on to include: (4) Not self-contradictory; capable of intellectual or esthetic development. The last seems to us a long way from *capable of living,* but there it is.

Many other words convey well meanings (3) and (4). *Viable* seems to us greatly overused nowadays in those meanings. See *viable* under **OVERUSED WORDS** for synonyms.

VIRGULE
1. Written prose is easy to read silently if it can be read comfortably aloud. Ordinary punctuation marks can be indicated orally, without actually naming them, by pauses, by dropping or raising the pitch of one's voice, and so on. The virgule—a slash—cannot be read aloud with any grace except when it is used to mean *divided by.* Its use to mean *and, or,*

or *and/or* makes a sentence awkward and frequently ambiguous. (See **AND/OR**.) Here are some examples.

It prevents council/board members from. . . . Easier to read
and quicker to grasp than that, it seems to us, is: *It prevents
members of councils and boards from. . . .* The latter seems to
us simple, clear, straightforward English syntax. No straining
of our imaginations brought forth any idea of what the author
of the original hoped to gain with the virgule.

"It is designed to aid people in their organization/helping
skills." Does that mean to aid people with their organizational
skills and also with their helping skills, or to aid them in
doing things in organizations and also to aid them with their
helping skills, or to aid their skill in helping organizations?
We are unable to decide. Our best guess is that the author
was substituting the virgule for a hyphen, and meant skill
in helping organizations, as in *skill in organization-helping.*
But if that was the author's intent, then *skill in helping
organizations* seems to us the simple way to say it. See
HYPHENS.

Pedagogical, economic, and political/school characteristics
. . . is written as if the author meant *political/school* to be a
unit of some sort, but that interpretation doesn't make sense.
We suppose the author meant the pedagogical, economic, and
political characteristics of schools. It seems to us that our
way of writing it is far easier to read than the way the author
wrote it. Here is another example that would read more
felicitously with commas and *and*: "At higher levels, an
individual can think more critically/logically/scientifically."

2. We see no advantage to substituting the virgule for the
hyphen, as we suspect the authors did in one or two of the
examples above. In much scientific and technical writing,
indeed, the substitution is impossible. The virgule is often
used to mean *divided by,* as in 3/4 or (a + b)/c. Person/
hour, as another example, means persons per hour, as through
a gate. To get the rate, you divide the number of persons

through the gate by the number of hours. In contrast, person-hours means the total count of units, each unit consisting of one person doing something for one hour. You multiply the number of persons by the number of hours. Those usages of the virgule and the hyphen are not interchangeable.

VISITATION: See **CONNOTATIONS.**

VITA: See **CURRICULUM VITAE.**

WHAT'S THAT AGAIN? We give examples here of some further ways writing can go awry.

1. **Garbled sentences.** One easy way to go astray is to put extra words between a preposition and its object: "Unobtrusive measures seem to be associated with, and induce a different set toward, data collection than is true for self-report measures." The author of that sentence obviously got off the main track (or back onto it?) after *with.*

Another way to go wrong is to forget the subject of the sentence: "The discovery of America was considered the new Garden of Eden." Presumably the author mean that it was America, not the discovery, that was the new Garden of Eden.

Another way is to forget what you wrote only four words before: "Some of the meteorites have been in the ice for more than a million years, possibly longer." Here is an example from Bernstein (under "Eh?"), along with his comment:

> "Of 789 British doctors who died in a twenty-nine month period, they said, death was attributed to lung cancer in thirty-five cases and contributed to death in a thirty-sixth case." There's no denying that death does make a great contribution to death.

2. **Mixed metaphors** are a never-ending source of delight. Here are a couple we have encountered, the first from an author who apparently thought Hercules was known for his complexity:

The complexity of this topic is Herculean.
The all-volunteer army is a sinking ship.

3. **Misquoted figures of speech.** Wrong words can creep into common figures of speech, often with entertaining results:

He sailed off into the unchartered seas of theory.
He wrapped his brains.
We met to flush out the plans.
The hatches are buttoned down.
Shoes and ships and ceiling wax.

Here are some choice examples from Bernstein (under "Curdled Clichés"):

It's in the lap of the cards.
They're trying to hurry to get under the gun.
He's a stiff shirt.
He muffed the boat.
The prisoner gave a facetious name.
They're cutting my throat behind my back.

4. **Malapropisms.** Sheridan made the name of Mrs. Malaprop forever famous by putting into her mouth, in his play *The Rivals*, one misused word after another. Here are some malapropisms we have come across:

Don't pour over the data.
He contacted the disease.
What you wrote in the last paragraph is diabolically opposed to what you wrote in this one.
Forward [the title of the introductory pages of a book].
The profound separation between professionals . . . was not easily breached.

5. So splendid is our last example that we do not presume to put a label on it. A student wrote to say that he had intended to return a book to one of us next time he was in town, but was sending it by mail, because "so far an occasion to come to Eugene has not arisen, and I think you are overduly deserving of the book being returned."

For more ways to confuse readers, see **ACTIVE AND PASSIVE VOICE; BRING WORDS TOGETHER THAT ACT TOGETHER; COMMA** 6; **CONNOTATIONS; DANGLERS; EACH, EVERY, ALL; GROUND ZERO; HYPHENS** 2; **MAXIMUM, MINIMUM; NOUNS AS ADJECTIVES; ORAL, VERBAL; PARALLELISM; POSITIVE, NEGATIVE; SHARE; TEND; THAT, WHICH; THIS, THAT;** and **WORDINESS.**

WHILE, SINCE: APA (p. 41) says flatly, "Do not use *while* in place of *although, whereas, and,* or *but.*" RHD and Webster III say just as flatly that using *while* to mean *whereas* or *although* is standard usage. The Ebbitts say that *"while* may mean 'although' or 'whereas,'" but the core of its meaning relates to time."

There is no denying that some writers do use *while* to mean *although, whereas, and,* and *but.* There is also no denying that some strange sentences result:

> Three students were going to be lost from the school's newspaper; one was graduating while two others were not working out.

When you mean *during the time that,* you can't get into trouble with *while*—as Bernstein, Baker, and Strunk and White take pains to point out. For other meanings, you might want to check whether *although, whereas, and,* or *but* would do better.

Since can make similar trouble. You can find yourself forgetting that *since* can mean *from then till now* as well as *because*:

> Since he had grown up in the Zincadian culture, he remained standing.

WHOLISM, WHOLISTIC: See **HOLISM, HOLISTIC.**

WILL: See **SHALL, WILL.**

WORDINESS: In an article about wordiness in scientific writing, David E. H. Jones (1980) quotes from a research report published in a scientific journal:

> It is common knowledge that contemporary man prefers to use his right hand when performing unimanual tasks; however, little evidence exists as to whether this has always been so. . . . To embark on such an investigation is theoretically important because it could possible elucidate the adequacy of competing explanations of the etiology of hand preference.

Jones's translation:

> Most people nowadays are right-handed. If we knew whether this has always been so, it would help us to understand why.

The chief objection to wordiness is not the cost of paper and type-setting, but that extra words are snags that get in the way of the reader. They make it hard to find the point of the sentence or paragraph. Spare writing is the more quickly and easily comprehended. Barzun (p. 20) says, "Ideas will best slide into a reader's mind when the word noise is least."

1. We did not invent the following examples; they actually appeared in print. After each, we offer a shorter version in brackets.

> Information was given through a lecture-type approach. [A lecture was given.] [See also **APPROACH.**]
>
> . . . to meet the requirement imposed by the fact of individual differences among learners. [. . . to cope with differences among learners.]
>
> Personnel would have to undergo significant retooling at the skills level. [Personnel would have to improve their skills significantly.]
>
> The technique of cluster analysis provides an approach to combining original data from separate studies into a single data set. [Cluster analysis uses data from separate studies as if the data came from a single set.]

Staff development should relate to the goals of the district as they are translated to student achievement. [Staff development should aid student achievement.]

Key issues with respect to the contested zone revolve around such questions as . . . [Key questions about the contested zone are . . .] [See **ABOUT.**]

Effort was focused on a single issue area. [We dealt with a single issue.]

My belief was that the district would have to develop the capacity to overcome problems on a continuing basis and that this would require the identification and training of personnel from within the system who could serve this purpose. [I believed the district needed a sustained capacity to overcome problems, but members of the district would need training.]

Leadership as a phenomenon is identifiable within its wider context as a form of action that seeks to shape its context. [Leaders seek to shape context.]

Abstractness makes wordiness even more opaque. Here are the words of an otherwise informal note a student wrote to a teacher:

Examination conditions of time constraints and output requirements present extreme difficulty with legibility for me.

That was a deep mystery, but the teacher at last deciphered it:

My handwriting gets very bad when I have to write an examination under a time limit.

2. Within sentences, phrases often contain unnecessary words:

Within a ten-minute time frame. [Within ten minutes.]
Observations of a less-sustained nature were made. [Less-sustained observations were made.]
Which is where the focus of this study is based. [Which is the focus of this study.]
Under conditions of small size in schools. [In small schools.]

Responsibility in the area of disciplinary problems. [Responsibility
for discipline.]
Meetings in which the members are principals. [Meetings of
principals.]

3. A phrasing that puts an elephantine rhythm into much
scholarly writing and increases its wordiness at the same time
is the gerund preceded by *the* and followed by *of:*

We began the planning of our schedule. [We began planning our
schedule.]
In addition to the developing of an accurate model. [In addition
to developing an accurate model.]
In the constructing of the questionnaire. [In constructing the
questionnaire.]

Another phrasing that makes writing heavy is the use of
the predicate adjective where the verb-form of the adjective
could replace *is:*

That finding is suggestive of. [That finding suggests.]
Johnson's article is responsive to recent criticism. [Johnson's article
responds to recent criticism.]
This paper is intended to be suggestive of. [This paper is intended
to suggest; I will suggest.]

4. *Basis* frequently encourages wordiness (see also **DAN-
GLERS**):

On a tentative basis. [Tentatively.]
On an on-going basis. [Continually, recurrently, regularly, etc.]
On a temporary basis. [Temporarily.]
On an as-needed basis. [As needed.]
On a three-week basis. [Every three weeks.]
They chose on the basis of their interest. [They chose what
interested them.]
Discussed on an informal basis. [Discussed informally.]
Organizing on a block-by-block basis. [Organizing block by block.]

5. Frequently, one or more words can simply be crossed
out. Omit the words in italics:

This is an emergency *situation*.
Used for fuel *purposes*.
He *is a man who* believes . . .
I was unaware *of the fact* that . . .
Johnson, *who is* an adherent of the same view . . .
In order to introduce the topic.
In *and of* itself.
The rate *which was* in the food box.
If *and when*.
A special difficulty was *the* time *element*.
The materials were complementary *in nature*.
The start-up *process* was lengthy.

6. Some writers like to make short words longer: *orientate* for *orient, burglarize* for *burgle, administrate* for *administer*. In England, a *minister* does the same things an *administrator* does in the United States.

7. A word that usually brings extra weight to prose is *which*:

The general living systems theory which this book presents is a conceptual system concerned primarily with concrete systems which exist in space-time. Complex structures which carry out living processes . . .

You can often extract *which*es and discard them:

The general theory of living systems this book presents is a conceptual system concerned primarily with concrete systems existing in space-time. Complex structures carrying out living processes . . .

See **THAT, WHICH**. See also **ELEGANT VARIATION, PUFFERY**, and **WHAT'S THAT AGAIN?**

WOULD HOPE: *Would*, as an auxiliary verb, as in *would hope, would do, would be*, is conditional; that is, it indicates that the hoping, doing, being, or whatever is not going on now, but would be under certain conditions: "I would do it if I had the time." "If we had studies of enough families in different socio-economic strata, I would then hope the problem could be quickly resolved." "Until more people understand the way they depend on the water table, I would not hope for political support." And so on.

Writers or speakers sometimes use *would hope* to mean simply *hope,* as in "I would hope we won't have to wait much longer." What the writer or speaker usually means is simply "I hope we won't have to wait much longer." If the *would* meant anything, we would expect a specification of some condition to follow, like "but, knowing the way Congress behaves in an election year, I can't allow myself the optimism." If there is no condition on the hoping, *would* should be omitted.

Similar remarks apply to *would* with any other verb: *suggest, seem, agree, like,* or whatever. For example, instead of *I would agree,* try *I agree.* Instead of *I would suggest to you,* try *I suggest, I propose, it seems to me, in my opinion.* Instead of *what I would like to describe is,* try *I will describe.* Instead of *I would like to present the following ideas,* try *I will present, I now present.*

ZERO: Don't get mixed up about nothing. The information that the quantity of something is zero is not the same as a lack of information. Sometimes a column in a table looks like this:

$$
\begin{array}{r}
23 \\
45 \\
17 \\
\hline
7 \\
5
\end{array}
$$

What does the dash mean? Does it mean that the column category was not applicable to that row category, or that the author could not get any information for that cell, or that the quantity there was zero? It is clearer, if the quantity is zero, to show a zero.

More References

Barclay, William R., M. Therese Southgate, and Robert W. Mayo. *Manual for Authors and Editors: Editorial Style and Manuscript Preparation.* Los Altos, California: Lange Medical Publications, 1981.

Berube, Margery S., Diane J. Neely, and Pamela B. DeVinne, eds. *American Heritage Dictionary: Second College Edition.* Boston: Houghton Mifflin, 1982.

Boulding, Kenneth E. "General Systems Theory—the Skeleton of Science." *Management Science* 2, no. 3 (1956): 197—208. Reprinted in W. Buckley, ed., *Modern Systems Theory for the Behavioral Scientist: A Sourcebook.* Chicago: Aldine, 1968. Pp. 3—10.

Bridgman, P. W. *The Logic of Modern Physics.* New York: Macmillan, 1927.

Campbell, D. T., and D. W. Fiske. "Convergent and Discriminant Validation by the Multitrait-Multimethod Matrix." *Psychological Bulletin* 56 (1959): 81—105.

Copi, Irving M. *Introduction to Logic.* 3rd ed. New York: Macmillan, 1968.

Council of Biology Editors Style Manual Committee. *Council of Biology Editors Style Manual: A Guide for Authors, Editors, and Publishers in the Biological Sciences.* 4th ed. Bethesda, Maryland: Council of Biology Editors, 1978.

Cronbach, Lee J., Nageswari Rajaratnam, and Goldine C. Gleser. "Theory of generalizability: A liberalization of reliability theory." *British Journal of Psychology* 16, no. 2 (1963): 137—63. See also L. J. Cronbach, G. C. Gleser, H. Nanda, and N. Rajaratnam. *The Dependability of Behavioral Measurements: Theory of Generalizability for Scores and Profiles.* New York: John Wiley, 1972.

Dobzhansky, Theodosius. *Mankind Evolving: The Evolution of the Human Species.* New Haven: Yale University Press, 1962.

Dyson, Freeman J. "Innovation in physics." *Scientific American* 199, no. 3 (1958): 74—82.

Encyclopedia of Psychology. Vol. 3 New York: Herder and Herder, 1972.

Fernald, James C. *Funk and Wagnalls' Standard Handbook of Synonyms, Antonyms, and Prepositions.* Rev. ed. New York: Funk and Wagnalls, 1947.

Hathwell, David, and A. W. Kenneth Metzner. *Style Manual for Guidance in the Preparation of Papers for Journals Published by the American Institute of Physics and Its Member Societies.* 3rd ed. New York: American Institute of Physics, 1978.

Jones, David E. H. "Last Word." *Omni* 2, no. 12 (1980): 130.

Kerschner, R. B., and L. R. Wilcox. *The Anatomy of Mathematics.* New York: Ronald Press, 1950.

Lewontin, Richard. *Human Diversity.* New York: W.H. Freeman, 1982.

McGrath, Joseph E., Joanne Martin, and Richard A. Kulka. *Judgment Calls in Research.* Beverly Hills, California: Sage, 1982.

Miller, James G. *Living Systems.* New York: McGraw-Hill, 1978.

Munson, Ronald. *The Way of Words: An Informal Logic.* Boston: Houghton Mifflin, 1976.

Runkel, Philip J., and Joseph E. McGrath. *Research on Human Behavior: A Systematic Guide to Method.* New York: Holt, Rinehart, & Winston, 1972.